Dylan Hall

This Life Ain't Gravy

Liwalo na Liwe

Published by Liwalo na Liwe

http://www.liwalo.org

Liwalo na Liwe Foundation
PO BOX 5091
Evanston, IL 60204-5091

Book Design by Jill Fenelon, Nathan Hall and Dylan Hall

ISBN 978-0-692-00052-6
LC Control Number 2008911318

December 2008

First Edition

Acknowledgments

It is hard for me to single out individual people to acknowledge. Some have kept me writing, others have encouraged me to go beyond my own limitations. Some have provided me with support my entire life. For you, I hope this book can serve as some positive reflection of your time and effort. You have made a difference.

Personally speaking, during my time with Justin, I often found myself praying for the strength to continue working with him. That source of support is what kept me going. And I would be remiss to fail to acknowledge it. Therefore, I do not really consider myself an author of this book but a mere transcriber of the events which seemed to have a higher purpose than myself. This is not to say that I have no connection with the book. I did write, edit and design it with the abilities that were given to me. Hopefully this explains the flaws within it, and I ask the reader to forgive these. Thank you.

If you see or hear goodness from me, then that goodness is from the Creator. You should be thankful to the Creator for all of that because I am not the architect of that; I am only the recipient. If you see weakness and shortcoming in me, it is from my own weakness and shortcoming. And I ask the Creator and the people to forgive me for that.

Mos Def

This Life Ain't Gravy

Chapter 1

First Visit

When I first met Justin, a 13 year-old African American male whom I was to mentor, I was surprised by his vulnerability. His previous mentor Lisa was graduating from the University of Illinois and moving away from Champaign, Illinois - Justin's hometown. At the time I was a junior at the same university and lived in Champaign as well.

Lisa took me to meet Justin at his house in the summer of 2006. The house looked run-down like most of the others that lined the busy Bradley Avenue in the predominantly Black neighborhood on the North Side of Champaign. Justin and his family lived on the second story of the house, and Lisa and I scaled wooden, exterior steps that led us from the ground to the second level. An Oldsmobile from the 1980's sat in the driveway. Lisa entered the house without knocking on the wooden door, turning a brass doorknob that surprisingly had no matching deadbolt lock for safety.

Inside, the house was not much to look at. Wooden floors and a lack of lighting gave the apartment a sense of darkness in the middle of a hot afternoon in June. Three bedrooms, eight feet by eight feet in size, were on the west side of the house. A kitchen and bathroom made up the east side, and a ten-foot hallway eventually led to the family room. Three boys were sleeping in the family room, one on a couch, another on an air mattress and a third on top of some blankets. One was Justin, and Lisa gingerly shook his shoulders to wake him up.

Justin might have been pulled out of the *Boondocks*. He had corn-rowed hair and was wearing a pair of gym shorts without a shirt on. He groaned while Lisa talked to him about meeting his new mentor. The other boys looked at me strangely. I returned the look, as this was a new experience for me. I had never been a mentor and did not have any experience working with youth. But there I was to help someone improve his life and to better understand the lives of teenagers like Justin. I believed that people were left behind in our society – that their gifts wasted for untold reasons. As a university student in Champaign, the opportunities were abundant and prospects bright. Ten minutes away from campus though, I believed there was a different story.

The house was worse than my college studio apartment in terms of condition, but the three boys sleeping on whatever they could was most shocking to me. For people from middle-class to upper-class backgrounds, seeing the realities of American poverty can be difficult, especially through the eyes of children. It challenged my notion of equal opportunity that grounded my confidence in American democracy. That first sight made me question whether or not I could have succeeded if I had grown up in that exact house, with nothing grand besides the television in the family room that was marred by a crack in its screen. Lisa seemed comfortable though. She spoke lightheartedly with the other boys in the room. They asked if they could go eat with Justin and the two of us, but she told them, "Not today."

Lisa had been mentoring Justin for at least a year without any connection to an organization. She met Justin through a friend who was a teacher at his school. Mostly, she would take Justin and his three other brothers to eat at a restaurant or to cook for them at her house. She also monitored Justin's performance at school. In preparing to leave Champaign, she requested four people from her church community to serve as mentors, one each for Justin and his brothers. I had been chosen to mentor Justin, the oldest and the one that she believed needed the most guidance - especially non-academic guidance.

Justin, Lisa and I went to lunch at a Chinese restaurant, and I tried to make conversation with Justin about basketball and rap music. Stereotypical as it may sound, I was trying to find his interests, and they were in fact these things. His favorite rapper was Lil' Wayne. He liked the Phoenix Suns professional basketball team. I suggested that we could play basketball the next time we got together. It was an awkward conversation at best, and often Justin and Lisa would talk personally about things only they knew about. Justin's demeanor was quiet and indifferent. In that sense, he reminded me of the teenager from the comic strip *Zits*.

After lunch, Justin and I made arrangements to meet again the following week. Lisa and I next visited her house. She confided that she thought Justin and I were a perfect pair because of my interest in basketball and rap music. Lisa also admitted that there was some barrier that she could not get over with Justin. She felt it was ultimately because she was a woman, and that Justin's adolescent stage might be better handled by someone of the same gender.

Before leaving I asked Lisa what she thought Justin needed most. She gave me a book about teaching children how to read and broke the news that Justin could not. If I could help him improve his reading, she thought that would possibly be my greatest role. Lisa also noted that Justin was raised only by his mother and that his father was in prison. The situation was simplistically stereotypical in light of these revelations. But the complexity would be discovered over the course of the next two years.

When looking at the needs of youth like Justin, they are often less complicated than the methods that are used to present them. Education, healthcare and money were an interpolation of needs – yet of those I could provide little. Justin also needed to have fun, to live life and to succeed. He needed to learn how to read. Quickly, my role was to become one of a guide as opposed to an inhibitor - something I had understood myself to be as a white person when I learned about historical and institutional racism in college. Perhaps most importantly, I made an effort to incorporate trust and reliability into our relationship, extending my perspective beyond racism and socioeconomic concerns. It helped me to overcome my own mental block of being overly concerned with these matters – as important as they were. This was a gift Justin gave me. For all that I would experience with him over the next two years, I feel more than compensated because he helped me find the heart I felt like I had lost, and I am forever indebted to him for it. Stop ∙

Our first week together, Justin and I attended the Champaign County Fair, riding rides and eating elephant ears in the overtly humid Midwestern summer day. As much as I wanted to teach him how to read, I thought it would be better to first establish a rapport. Our relationship initially was antagonistic as he dominated me in Bumper Cars, pinning me up against the wall several times. It turned humorous while he screamed with fear on the pirate ship, eventually vowing while walking to never ride the ride again. The relationship briefly became racial when a young white boy, about eight years old, was walking straight towards us but looking off to the side. Then, turning his head to look straight at us, he became frightened of Justin. The boy's eyes were wide, and he stood still as if he had happened upon a snake. We kept walking, and Justin asked laughingly, "What's wrong with him?"

I told him I did not know, and we started talking about bumper cars as Justin again gloated over his victories, continuing the antagonism. The child's reaction seemed insignificant at the time. He might have been reacting to something his parents said or images he had seen on the television, and it caused him to be afraid. It was an unbridled response as children are wanton to do.

Regardless, Justin was perceived as dangerous. Maybe it was from the baggy shorts or the oversized t-shirt that he wore in combination with the color of his skin. It was a small incident.

Its importance was not that the child was some racist or that Justin was ultimately hurt. Rather, it was revealing of a greater contradiction. Some people already believe Justin is dangerous, a threat who has no desire to improve himself. If he fails, it is ultimately a condemnation of his character. But it is expected. To tell someone he or she has potential but secretly believe that there is no chance for success is ultimately a problem. Achievement is an exception, and one is left to wonder if there is ever really a clean slate with which people are viewed when even an eight-year old cannot look at a smiling Black teenager without judgment.

This book is a story about Justin. I tried my hardest to provide him with a clean slate, to not judge him, his family, his race or class. Ultimately condemnation would come about for both of us, but I believe it never fell under any of those categories. His story is worth telling, not for the successes or the failures in it, but rather because it is simply his story. Hopefully it will provide you with greater insight into some of the challenges that confront us as people in the twenty-first century.

Chapter 2

Friends

As with the county fair, Justin and I continued to enjoy the summer months. I took Justin driving and played catch with him. It was a honeymoon stage of sorts, as we did relatively little work on his reading. I also took Justin to the university recreation center – a place he thought to be no less than paradise upon first visit.

Justin was not scared of the college environment at the recreational center. He would join in the pick-up basketball games or shoot hoops in the swimming pool with other university students. They were usually surprised as Justin would run up to them and begin playing without even a word; it seemed given the right opportunity, Justin would take advantage of it. When we played basketball together in the swimming pool, we would usually trash talk each other. He would tackle me when I would go up to dunk on the hoop, and I would reject his shots. Every time he claimed to have won, but I knew the truth.

Our times at the mall were always interesting. Justin and I often argued over whether or not he should get a grill. A grill is something that rappers have made popular. It is put in a person's mouth and covers the teeth. Often, it is lined with fake gold or diamonds. To me it seemed ridiculous, reminiscent of my braces in high school, but to Justin it was cool. I told him, "You have your style, and I have mine. I will help you buy the things you need, but a grill is not something you need."

Later Justin would thank me for not buying him one. I knew that Justin would probably never look like me in terms of style or find the same things important at that moment, but I wanted to be there to help him make better decisions with the pursuits that he chose. Once while he and his friends were shopping for sunglasses, Justin's friend read "Coach" on a sign above a row of sunglasses. He could not believe that "Coach" sunglasses were so cheap. I read the fine print and told him that above "Coach" it said "Made to look like." He was disappointed and walked away from the cheap imitations.

Justin's best friend was Calvin. He was white and lived down the street from Justin. Calvin was mostly quiet and displayed what is referred to as the "cool pose" perhaps better than any of his Black friends. The cool pose is marked by toughness displayed through indifference. Slow walking, head sometimes down and almost no facial expression, Calvin also dressed well. He had the whitest shoes, designer jeans and oversized t-shirts that were colorful with elaborate patterns. He had an MP3 player, the major mark of status at that time as cell phones were not new anymore. Anything Calvin owned, I believe Justin would have wanted for himself, especially since Justin had almost nothing. Every so often, Calvin's mother would take trips to go shopping in nearby cities like Chicago and would take Calvin and Justin with her. She might help Justin buy dinner or get some inexpensive clothes. I wondered if being around Calvin's family's lifestyle left Justin feeling inadequate, or if he was friends with Calvin exactly because of this inadequacy. Was it a hindrance to their friendship or a motivation for it?

Calvin also helped Justin join MySpace, a social networking website. On MySpace, every member has a profile which contains the person's picture, a description of the person as well as a listing of his or her friends who also belong to MySpace. Justin's profile had a picture of Calvin and Justin standing together in a cool pose and making the symbol M.O.B. with their hands. M.O.B. or "Money Over Bitches" represents the belief that money is the most important thing in this world and nothing should come between a man and his wealth, not even a woman. This picture embodied an aspect of popular culture for youth that spoke to materialism. Justin once showed me a person on MySpace who had made a video about the clothes in his closet and the one-hundred pairs of shoes he owned. Justin was envious. I then showed Justin a video about Jackie Robinson, to which he was indifferent. "I do not care about the past," he said.

I could never interest Justin in African American history. He knew about Dr. Martin Luther King Jr., Malcolm X, Harriet Tubman and others famous personages but felt they were irrelevant to him in daily life.

It was disheartening for me, but it did not make me think less of Justin. Justin was worried about clothes, but how many teenagers were not? In shopping malls across the country, numerous teenagers were probably spending money and time that could be better utilized elsewhere. It was not something endemic to Justin, his race or even his class. Rather, Justin's problems made his obsession with clothes seem more problematic simply because he had so little. It is similar to being asked by someone with an untreated, gaping wound if he or she could have an ice pack for a jammed finger. People outside of Justin's circumstances might see that his passion for clothes could be better placed elsewhere and they might be correct, but such understandings can create their own problems when the youth is labeled negatively for trying to fix the finger all the while unaware of the larger wound.

Justin was also one of many competing against advertisers with college degrees targeting a consumer model that he fit exactly. Why did Justin want the things he did? He came to understand that they were important through advertising and peer pressure. The people who made the letters "Coach" large and "Made to look like" small knew what they were doing. Justin was not a helpless victim, but he, like any other child, simply needed someone to provide different perspective. Justin's friend Calvin also bought into the hype of fashion, but I did not dislike Calvin for participating in that interest or think that he was a bad friend for Justin to have. Justin most likely would have had the same clothes and accessories as Calvin had he had the means to acquire them.

Justin's "cousin" JT was another friend whom I met. He, Justin and I went to the university recreational center to play basketball on a summer afternoon. JT was talented and hit outside jump shots easily. I thought he could have a future in basketball if had the desire. He even beat me in a game. In addition to mentoring, I began practicing basketball over the summer to make sure it would not happen again.

On the drive home, Justin and JT were talking about girls and fights they had gotten into over the course of their lives. Justin was bragging about one fight with his brother and then revealed to JT that he had once hit his mother as she tried to separate him and his brother. JT said, "You hit your mom man? I could never do that. That ain't right."

Justin was embarrassed and changed the subject of the conversation. His older friend had set a standard that he did not live up to. I did not believe Justin and I had developed a close enough bond where I could reprimand him for something and actually make him think about it. Seemingly inherently, I knew to never hit my mother, but Justin clearly did not have this understanding. It made me question the cause. Did he not like his mother, someone whom I had not yet met at the time with the exception of a brief introduction, or was he really caught up in the moment of fighting? Maybe he had witnessed other men hit women causing such an act seem acceptable. It was important to find a cause if one existed instead of just condemning his action.

As we became more familiar with each other, Justin and I began reading practice towards the end of the summer. We used the instructional book Lisa had given me and went over the basic phonics of reading. Even though Justin knew the sounds of most letters, he did not know short vowel sounds. Sounds of the consonants "w" and "l" he struggled with as well. Mostly, Justin was familiarized with sight words, and as we would read books together, I found that he could not sound out unfamiliar words. We made small increments of progress though. When we were driving past restaurants, he would sound out the words on the signs. Once, when I was parking on the side of a street, he sounded out, "No Pa-king."

By August 2007, Justin's eighth grade year had started, and we continued the routine of reading. I picked up Justin from his middle school instead of his house. Every Friday, the bell would ring and children came running down the stairs. A staff member with a megaphone would try to herd the children into the auditorium. "Bus riders! The buses are leaving in five minutes! Five minutes bus riders!"

A shorter woman with a loud voice would yell at those children who were running in the hallways or wearing a hat. A security officer strolled in an authoritative manner as children were careful to keep their distance, even though they would talk to him without giving it much thought. Boys would run after the girls and pull on their book bags. Girls would speak loudly, looking around to see if anyone else was listening to their story. Calvin usually recognized me from a distance and passed by without acknowledgment. Justin would approach laughing with a group of friends or sometimes quietly by himself if he had not had a good day.

I could tell it made him feel important to have someone waiting for him, so I did so every Friday for the entire school year. He had three younger brothers and his mother was taking care of all four of the boys by herself. As a result, I doubted many people went out of their way to wait on Justin or provide him with individual attention, and for me to do so might have helped to give him a sense of worth.

Justin's school stood directly across from the Champaign Public Library. Often Justin's friends would walk with us to the parking lot on their way to the library and occasionally one would ask to come along with us. It was interesting because these boys usually tried to act tough, they themselves a part of the "M.O.B" clique. Frequently they were shy and hesitant to ask to tag along, often leaving Justin to ask the question and offering a "Thank you," if I said yes.

Our first action was to go and eat dinner at some fast-food restaurant like McDonald's. I would pay for Justin and whoever else was with us. The friend was usually surprised and expressed gratitude. It showed that the boys did not come along to receive anything. They might have just wanted attention or to be around someone older. They understood though that I could not bring them along every week. Regardless, I spent a day with most of Justin's friends by the time I had left Champaign.

Interestingly, it seemed every time I dropped off a friend at his house, the friend told me he wanted a mentor too and asked if I knew of anyone who could be his. The truth was that I did not know of anyone. Even at a large institution like the University of Illinois, student interest was low. Students were busy with school, organizations, jobs, and socializing. Still, it was disappointing. Perhaps most difficult to witness were the students who were blasting rap music at parties at night and throwing up gang signs in pictures. If they really wanted to live the hard-nosed gangster lifestyle, they could have seen it through the eyes of a youth going through what those songs talk about, often ten minutes away from where that party was at. Justin's friends showed me that they wanted help, but that few people were stepping up. Even if it was one day a week, many students could have made a difference in the

Champaign community. For many students though, the thought never crossed their minds.

Realizing this, I faced an issue that encompassed separating my work with Justin from my personal life. The mentoring experience began to change my perspective on college and life. In light of his struggles, much of what was associated with college seemed frivolous. It impacted me in a negative manner as I became overly critical of the college environment around me, refusing to take part in most of it. In reflection, I now know a balance needed to be found. It took me the full two years to do so. Regardless, I offer this personal reflection not for sympathy, but to provide a glimpse into the challenges inherent in my mentoring experience. It was not always easy.

One of Justin's friends in particular stood out. Daryl was a big, quick basketball player in Justin's class. He was outgoing with his friends, fearless on the basketball court, confident in his demeanor, and he came along with Justin for two consecutive weeks. Strangely, he was nervous around me, often unsure of what to say. His voice would become quiet and he would look to the ground when I asked him a question. By the second week I think he found enough strength to ask me if I knew of anyone who could spend time with him. Daryl was not in dire straits financially according to Justin, but he lived in a single-parent home and I think he was looking for an older male to fill something that was missing from his life. It was amazing to see how his personality transformed when he was around me - more so than in any of Justin's other friends. I could not give him what he wanted though and did not know anyone else who could do so. It was disappointing to say the least. Particularly perplexing was the fact that if he was solely to be judged based upon his persona amongst his friends, he would have seemed fine. But he felt something was missing. Again, many of those youth wanted someone in their lives. Daryl embodied

13

strength amongst his friends, but even he had weaknesses underneath it all. For the one Justin I was with, there were many more wanting something similar.

Despite those difficulties, I had fun watching Justin and his friends interact. One night, I took Justin and three friends to a roller skating rink. It was the happening place for the eighth graders to be. Rap music was blaring through the speakers and intricate lighting sequences gave the skating rink a disco feel. Songs that had particular dances tied to them were received with much enthusiasm as four year-olds to teenagers performed the steps in unison amongst exultations of excitement. Calvin did not dance, instead choosing to sit at a table and listen to his MP3 player. Justin confided to me that he did not understand why Calvin was at the skating rink.

I skated around by myself and tried not to fall. Justin and his other friends tore through the rink, scaring girls, barely missing them as they swept by. Back and forth Justin and his friends would skate between the arcade and the skating rink. One of the girls stole Justin's hat, causing a big uproar and much verbal sparring as Justin and his friends pitted themselves against the girl and her friends. Eventually an employee settled the matter. It was sheer junior high madness.

I look back fondly at this time. As certain situations developed, Justin and I came to spend more one-on-one time, and we still had fun – albeit different. It seemed he lost the joy that he displayed so easily at this time. He matured past the junior high stage of life and started to assert himself as an adult. He would also have to confront situations which he did not at this time. Perhaps it was that transition into becoming an adult or that society reacted to him differently since he was viewed no longer as a Black youth but rather a young Black man. Maybe it was the increasing of expectations as his age necessitated, but regardless, some great weight had fallen on him, much like

I had done after an hour on the skating rink floor. Justin never let me forget that and never will.

Chapter 3

Basketball

With winter approaching, I encouraged Justin to try out for the junior high basketball team. Even though we were working on reading at least once a week, he was still spending most of his time with his friends – probably not being very productive. I believed the basketball team would give him a chance to do something he enjoyed, keep him out of trouble and help him develop some basic team skills. He wanted to as well and made the early-morning tryouts with the help of Calvin's mother.

I saw Justin the first Friday following the tryouts, and he was upset. He did not make the team, but most of his friends had. Justin blamed the coach for being cut. He was placed on the weaker team in a two-team scrimmage and felt that he could not impress the coach as a result. Justin's mother Natasha visited the coach; he told her that Justin's problem was one of attitude. I was frustrated to see an opportunity lost, but the coach must have seen Justin as unmanageable since he did have raw talent. He was a better player than many of his friends whom I played basketball against and who made team.

Instead, Natasha and I signed up Justin for a YMCA basketball team. The YMCA had an eighth-grade league that held games every Saturday and practices at least once a week. Although it would not provide the same experience as junior high basketball, it could serve as a bridge to high school if he wanted to try out for basketball again. Programs like the YMCA league are valuable because they provide opportunities for youth to continue their involvement with a sport or activity. Justin's raw talent may have been unappealing for a coach who wanted to win that year, but in a few years he would most likely be taller and stronger than his peers that had made the eighth grade team. Not being able to play that year could stunt his development or desire and both of these possibilities could have damaging effects. The coach's decision was justifiable, especially because of his attitude concerns, but the YMCA league served as a great resource.

The only advice I gave Justin when he signed up for the league was to always hustle and listen to the coach. If a player fails while following the coach's rules, it is the coach's fault. If a player fails while hustling, his or her desire cannot be questioned.

Desire, Justin definitely possessed. The first sight I had of him before a game in the YMCA basketball gymnasium was no different than what he had displayed in the campus recreational center. He joked around with each of his teammates, laughing and waiting for his turn in line to do a lay-up or get a rebound.

I sat down on the metal, three-rowed bleachers that were pushed back against the gymnasium wall. The gymnasium itself was dilapidated. Several of the areas on the wooden floor were dead spots on which the ball could not rise any higher than one foot if dribbled there. The large glass windows on the northern side had lost their opacity with time. Still, the weathered basketball court would do, and perhaps it even enhanced the experience as it hearkened back to the fading days of short shorts, mid-range jump shots and underhanded free throws.

Justin acknowledged my presence by nodding his head, and I responded in the same manner. Shooting before the game, he would look over at times to see if I had been watching when he made a shot. I was quick to look away just before he did in order to prevent him from trying to impress me. Eventually, the coach called the players in to huddle before the start of the game. Justin casually walked to the huddle with his arm around a newfound friend and teammate.

The game was fun to watch. The family members in attendance, especially the mothers, provided their loved ones enthusiastic disbelief when a shot was made, anger when a foul was inflicted and sympathy when the ball was turned over to the other team. Justin was an impressive player. He could jump higher than most players on the floor and would get many rebounds. He had big hands and long arms and would bat down the passes of his frustrated opponents. On offense, he would usually shoot close to the basket making about half of his shots. When he stole the ball from opponents he would bring it up the court as fast as he could and pass to one of his teammates to set up a good shot. He was a good dribbler for being relatively tall in comparison to the other players on the floor. Especially engaging was his demeanor when he played. While some players played scared, others aloof, Justin played with enthusiasm, seemingly happy to just have an opportunity to play. His enthusiasm bridled over into the laps of his teammates' parents, who soaked it up and remarked positively upon the passion with which he played.

Justin's excitement was rarely tempered, but his interactions with the coach often affected his normally buoyant temperament. During one throw-in by the opposing team, Justin's coach repeatedly told Justin to move closer to the basket in order to get into the proper defensive position. The coach took Justin out of the game after that play to better explain what he wanted during the throw-in, but for someone who displayed such joy in playing, benching was the greatest punishment, even if it was not intended to be. When the coach called time-out with Justin still on the bench, the team huddled together, except for Justin who preferred to maintain his seat. His response to the perceived punishment created a true punishment as the coach sat him for the entire quarter, refusing to play someone who would not get up to be with his teammates and take part in the team huddle.

After the game, Justin complained about the coach. "How can he sit me out when the other team is making a run? They made that run right when he took me out, and they won 'cause he wouldn't put me back in."

He was right that the opposing team made the run when he was sitting on the bench, but I countered that a player could not disrespect the team like he had done. The coach sat him probably because he did just that. Particularly contradictory was the fact that Justin did it out of love for the game of basketball. He wanted to play. He wanted to win. He just wanted to do so in his own manner. He did not sit on the bench in protest because he did not like his teammates but because he did not like his coach.

As the season progressed, this scenario played out seemingly over and over again. Justin simply could not do what the coach told him if he did not agree with it. His attitude decreased his playing time, and it also made a negative impression on some of the parents and other family members who had initially viewed him with such great favor. One woman who knew Justin's mother Natasha casually did not blame Justin for his actions but instead his family situation. "She does not have it all together," the woman confided to me about Natasha.

Thus, I found people could hold a dualistic view of Justin. At times he was a talented basketball player with great enthusiasm. Otherwise, he was a behaviorally challenged, problematic youth. The woman's explanation gave me the impression that Justin could not change since his actions stemmed from external causes. I too was disappointed with his relationship with the coach, and I spoke with Justin after each game about the proper way to play on a team. My frustration then lay not with Justin's mother but with Justin himself as he failed to make changes in how he dealt with the coach. It seemed the woman used Justin's performance on the court to serve a personal agenda that was none too helpful to Justin or his mother.

While Justin was playing a basketball game on the court, the woman was playing the blame game in the stands. The blame was probably made out of the frustration of seeing Justin struggle despite having so much potential, but it was mostly ineffectual for bringing about change.

Natasha told me that she would not attend Justin's games until Justin treated her with respect and followed the rules of the house. The problems with his coach seemed to parallel those with his mother, as he did not want to live up to her expectations either. Justin complained that his mother would not even come to one of his games like "she is supposed to."

A greater sign of disharmony emerged when Justin told me he had moved to his aunt's house midway through the season. The move was temporary from Natasha's perspective and permanent from Justin's. Eventually, something would have to give, but an artificial equilibrium was reached. The situation was a significant development in Justin's life, but I was unsure about what I should have done in my role as a mentor. I focused on helping Justin on the basketball court and in his reading, hopeful that the family issue would be resolved internally, without some outsider barging in.

As for basketball, it was interesting that as the only Black player on the team, Justin seemed to also be the only player to have a conflict with his Black coach. The coach was not condescending towards Justin's abilities but only towards Justin's attitude. After one loss, the coach gathered the players together for what I assumed to be an "it's now or never" talk for the underachieving team. Justin looked to the ground while the coach spoke, and after the coach had finished, acted as if he had just been "chewed out" by heading to my car with his head still down and pace steadily slow. We ran into the coach in the parking lot. He looked at Justin and said, "When I was talking [after the game] about the two players on our team who could play college ball, one of them was you. I have been coaching for thirty years and I have had two former players go past college to the pros, so I know what I am talking about. But first you have to get your attitude straight. You have to decide what you are going to be and what you want to be. You have all the talent in the world, but if you do not want it for yourself, you will never be as good a basketball player as you can be."

Justin listened attentively as these remarkable words were offered to him. It felt as if this moment was a breakthrough, the stuff movies were made of. But after the coach departed, Justin told me yet again that he did not like him. A compliment was lost because of the messenger. I could not believe Justin's indifferent reaction.

From Justin's perspective, however, he had been cut from a junior high basketball team and told that he could be a college basketball player. It probably did not add up in his mind and showed why words could only accomplish so much. Regardless, in both situations his attitude was determined to be the major roadblock. His YMCA coach said that Justin needed to decide for himself what he wanted. Watching him on the court, I knew he loved the game of basketball and playing with other players his age. As Justin's mentor, I felt the responsibility to help him develop his character and basketball could have perhaps been the best tool to do so.

While sports like basketball are often perceived as competition in opposition against another, they can also be a method for individual definition in the battle against oneself. The mirror images of the struggles Justin had between his coach and his mother spoke to a need to adapt or modify his behavior in certain situations. Since my words seemed to have at least some impact on Justin, I offered Justin the opportunity to practice basketball with me early in the morning before school. He was hesitant because of the morning hour, but he told me he wanted to be a good basketball player. Eventually, he agreed. He was most happy about having one-on-one time I believe.

For our first training session, I drove ten minutes to Justin's temporary residence at 6 A.M. on a weekday morning unsure if he would want to wake up in the midst of the cold of winter. Justin's aunt opened the door and told Justin to get ready. He was sleeping on an air mattress on the family room floor while a Nickelodeon cartoon played on the television in the background. I stood at the door. Justin gathered his practice clothes and school clothes. His aunt signed a form for Justin's YMCA membership. We were going to practice at the same gymnasium he played his games at.

We arrived at the YMCA and had our membership photos taken. The photos resembled mug shots because of the early hour; I think we were nearly prohibited from membership because of them. The staff let us into the gymnasium regardless, and the training began. Justin took my basketball and did warm-up shots while I stretched. After five minutes of shooting, I put on my coach's face and we began to go through drills. The first drill was to be a simple pass back-and-forth as we shuffled our feet and moved up and down the court. Justin briefly smiled while I explained the drill then quickly hid the smile, trying to match my serious expression. Next we worked on post moves and free throws. We were in the process of doing sprints when Justin started to jog with little effort. I told him he needed to speed up his pace, but he told me he was having trouble breathing because he had asthma and had forgotten his inhaler. That ended the session. He had performed well and definitely did have potential.

Two days later I went to his aunt's house again at the same early hour but no one answered the door. I saw Justin later that week for our regularly scheduled Friday, and he admitted that he failed to wake up. I suspected that Justin was not interested in playing basketball to improve but simply just for fun. The next week he failed to wake up twice more, and I told him that we were finished with practicing for the time being. I was not disappointed in him, but the experience helped me to understand what Justin wanted and needed. The problems with his mother had brought a huge weight on his shoulders, and it seemed that they needed to be resolved before anything else positive could come about for Justin. He just did not need me to be a basketball coach. Rather, he most likely needed someone to become more involved in his family and to help him bridge whatever divide existed between he and his mother.

Yet Justin could still play basketball and enjoy the opportunity to have fun. He finished out the YMCA season strong and even though he still had conflicts with his coach, they were of a lesser magnitude. Eventually, enough players had started to miss games and practices that sitting out Justin was impossible. Unlike most of his teammates, Justin always wanted to be at the game - making the thirty minute bicycle ride in the winter without someone prodding him to go. While basketball may have been an obligation for those players who missed the games, it was a relief for Justin, away from the confusion of his living and family situation. The extra effort he made to be ordinary clued me into the meaning of the word extraordinary, and while players were often praised for their athletic ability, I found Justin to be more than a basketball player. He was a teenager with great resolve in light of the situations he confronted – shouldering at that time the drama of a soap opera in his quest for happiness. Unfortunately, the story was just unfolding.

Chapter 4

Conflict

Finishing the YMCA basketball season had blown us into the winds of March 2007. The uncertainty of Justin's living arrangement had been resolved. Justin's uncle forced him to move back home with Natasha and his brothers. The uncle suspected that Justin had stolen something from his cousin, and Justin, not afraid to stand up for himself when he believed was innocent, did just that. The defiance bothered the uncle so much that he told his wife, Justin's aunt, that it was either he or Justin who would stay in the house - but not both. The aunt made the decision quickly and Justin went home.

Justin was not happy to return home. Living with three younger, antagonizing brothers in such a small living space upset Justin, and his retaliations were not of indifference but of action, often drawing the ire of Natasha. Once while I was waiting in Justin's room for Justin to get dressed to go with me for the day, Justin went in search of a pair of socks. His ten year-old brother Randall followed him into the room and stood in Justin's way in an effort to draw his attention. Justin tried to push Randall to the side and out of his way, but since Randall was standing in an off-balance manner, Randall fell to the ground. Hearing the thud, Natasha ran into the room, saw Randall on the floor and said, "Don't touch my son! What are you doing pushing my boy around?"

"He's bothering me! I was just trying to get some socks and he keeps messing with me!" Justin retorted.

Natasha told him he was the oldest and he should be setting an example, "not acting like a ten year-old."

Since he could not be mature, she told him he could not come with me that day. Justin stormed into his room and yelled at Natasha, making it clear that he hated living in the house and wanted to leave. I followed Justin into his room and sat with him on his bed. Justin had his back towards me, with his eyes looking outside the window that faced the north-south street that passed by their house. There was so much anger in him, as tears built up in his eyes and he sat quietly, like the silence before a storm. Similar to the basketball games, now his mother was the coach and the bed the bench where he thought he sat alone. I believed I needed to show him how rationally confronting the issue would lead to a better outcome than what sheer anger could produce. After some time Justin admitted that he and his mother had been arguing about a different matter that had occurred prior to that day.

Two days earlier Justin had been outside of his house, fixing a bicycle in his backyard when his cousin stopped by. The cousin asked Justin if he could go inside Justin's house to get a drink of water. Justin let him. Unknown to Justin though, the cousin hid inside the house a plastic bag that contained an illegal drug. His cousin came back outside, and Justin walked with him on the streets to pass the time – at least in Justin's understanding. Instead, Justin found himself in the middle of a drug deal being conducted by his cousin, someone who was a year younger than him.

Justin kept a limited distance while the deal took place. He went home afterwards and found a confrontational Natasha who had discovered the hidden bag. As Justin recounted the events of that day to Natasha, she was disgusted that he had been taken advantage of by someone younger than him. She said his cousin was not his friend but an opportunist using people for his own gain. But Justin defended spending time with his cousin since they were kin. Justin thought he was being a good cousin, Natasha thought Justin was being naïve and putting himself in danger.

After recounting the events of the past two days, Justin told me his mother did not care about him. She only cared about his brothers he thought. I asked Justin why he thought his mother was worried about him spending time with his cousin. He did not know. I suggested that she did not want Justin to be influenced by his cousin because she was concerned about him. Instead of being angry at his mother, I told Justin he should be angry at his cousin; he was the one who had taken advantage of Justin and left drugs where the people Justin cared about could find them. His mother had shown more concern for him than his cousin had, but Justin thought the opposite held in the strained social contract that existed between the teenage boys.

Eventually Natasha came into the room. She explained why she was upset with Justin, afraid that he was on track to become his cousin, someone who had run away from home and dropped out of school. She was also mad that Justin hurt her son Randall, just as she was mad when her nephew had potentially hurt her sons, taking one to a drug deal and leaving all with an unwelcome surprise in their house. She told Justin he could go with me for the day, and even though Justin listened with relief woven into his face, he still would not apologize to his mother. I told him to do so, but he refused, and walking out the door, Natasha said, "Don't worry about it Dylan."

Flushed with the experience of one mediation, I was optimistic that improvement could be perpetual and success eventual. Even though Justin would not apologize to his mother, he might have begun to understand that his mother did care about him - something which he earlier denied so vehemently. Unfortunately, as time went on, Justin's burden became heavier.

The added weight began as school was nearing dismissal for summer vacation. For two weeks, I could not find Justin at his school or at his house. Also, his family was not connected to a phone line or the internet, and not even a cellular phone provided a means of communication at the time. Essential for certain aspects of life, but not ultimately for life, these social amenities were lost when food was lacking or money was tight for Natasha. Thus, some weeks would simply be lost as Justin and I would not see each other.

By the third week, I found Natasha at their house; she explained Justin was placed in the juvenile detention center after an altercation with his thirteen year-old brother Lawon. They fought over what Natasha described to be a, "white, dingy t-shirt."

Justin was upset because Lawon borrowed the t-shirt without Justin's permission. Fist fighting broke out amongst the boys, and Natasha's friend found the two boys rolling around on the hallway floor. Trying to separate the combatants, the friend called for Natasha's help. Heeding her words and cries, the boys came to a stopping point, and Natasha's friend took Lawon outside. Natasha held Justin to the floor and tried to calm him down. Thinking that Justin had finally succumbed to rationale, she let him stand up, and Justin bolted down the stairs and pushed Lawon against the beat-up Oldsmobile that sat in the driveway. Natasha's friend called the police, and Natasha hit Justin on his back with a heel in order to get him to stop fighting, as she feared for Lawon's safety. The police were at the house within a manner of minutes and took Justin to the detention center.

"Huh?" was my initial reaction. This was serious. This was dangerous. This was stupid. But this was reality - a side of Justin I had not seen. And the fact that a situation such as this one existed suggested that I should not shy away from it. The fight was not simply about a t-shirt. In existence were probably a multitude of sociological and psychological reasons. But my simplest understanding was in the value that Justin attached to clothes, not because he was greedy or vain, but because they provided him with a sense of value in return. The same worth someone can give another in the name of love was provided by clothes for Justin. Just as two people may fight over one lover who is not treating either person well, so could Justin become upset over a dirty, white t-shirt. In my life I had been just as guilty of overvaluing something that cradled my self-worth.

The reality that confronted me then was that I had accomplished very little with Justin. He missed his graduation, as a time for celebration turned into a visitation to the detention center. The complexity of the situation seemed better handled by someone else. But who else was there? Justin refused to accept Natasha's phone call and even her visit to the detention center. Their relationship seemed to deteriorate rapidly. I did not want Justin to believe that the world had passed him by so quickly - offering indifference when he needed something more. He had talents and strengths, and I decided I would make every effort to help him. I started by scheduling a visit with Justin.

I arrived at the Champaign County detention center in the beginning of June. A clean, brick building hidden on the eastern side of the city of Urbana, it stood next to the county nursing home, jail and park district gymnasium. I opened the exterior doors to the detention center and stood in the entranceway, where I happened upon another set of doors - these locked. I was called upon by someone through an intercom. The person asked for the purpose of my entrance into the building. I responded that I had come to visit Justin, and a clicking sound keyed me to enter the second set of doors, now unlocked.

In the lobby green metal benches faced the main office. A wall with a window separated the lobby and the office, and a slot underneath the window allowed for the passing of materials from one room to the other. Another voice emanated from the direction of the window and asked why I was in the lobby. I restated my purpose. The door to the main office was opened. The experience was good practice for a trial before God if such a thing existed. All I needed was a purpose and an unknown figure would unlock the doors for me.

In the office, a tall, balding man said he had not been expecting any visitors. Another woman came to the desk and told him that she had forgotten to put my visit into the system. The man made me put my keys and loose change in a locker and led me to the visiting room. Concrete, cylinder block walls did not infuse the building with a sense of warmth. Neither did the silver metal door through which we passed on our way to the visitation room. A second door and finally a third door led me into the contact room where Justin was to be brought in shortly. Two buttons and an intercom were on a panel on the wall. "Press this button when you are ready to leave. The red button is a panic button. Press that if you have any problems," the man said in departure, smiling at me.

His effort at reassurance was half-hearted. I did not expect to use the red button nor fear for my safety, but the drabness of the detention center frightened me with the possibility of failure, especially when Justin entered the room escorted by a guard.

Justin's long hair stood straight on end, and he wore a blue sweatshirt and grey sweatpants and slipper-shoes. He slouched in his chair with his legs off to the side. I told Justin that even though he was in the detention center, he was not a bad person and asked him to honestly tell me what had happened. His story mostly matched Natasha's - just from a different perspective. In addition, he blamed Lawon for starting the fight and sought to disown his own home. "I don't wanna go back there. I'm going to live at my auntie's house. I want you to have my mom put all of my clothes in a box and take it to my auntie's, so no one can wear them."

He did not want anyone wearing those clothes. Twice he interrupted his recollection of the fight to ask me to ensure that his clothes were not touched. There he sat in the juvenile detention center at age fourteen, and his biggest concern was a pair of jeans and some t-shirts. But teenagers are like that. A cell phone, car and clothes all take on an added importance in junior high and high school as social expectations sometimes conflict with future aspirations. The fact that Justin sat in the detention center made his immaturity seem too great though. Many teenagers would make every effort to avoid or remedy such a situation out of respect for oneself or one's family, but the idea of incarceration and delinquency was a common theme in Justin's neighborhood and in his family particularly. His father was incarcerated in Illinois, and Natasha said she spoke often with her children about the necessity to avoid the legal system. I never had those discussions with my family, but in a country where one in fifteen Black men are in prison compared with one in 100 adult men overall, such a difference is not atypical. Mostly, I wondered if Justin would be able to think about his future if he at least led a comfortable life, where possessions were perhaps more abundant and thereby rendered less important.

Justin admitted that he refused his mother's visit. He did not want to see her because he felt victimized. He was convinced that the unpunished Lawon bore the mark of the favored one, and that Justin was placed in the detention center because his family did not want him around. I told Justin that he needed to take the time to improve his reading instead of simply being angry. He revealed he had already borrowed the book *Charlie and the Chocolate Factory* from the detention center library. The library limited time with a book to three days for each juvenile, so he did not get to read it to completion, but reading was a step he had already taken on his own.

His public defender had also visited him and said he should be released next week when his hearing was held in the Champaign County Courthouse. I promised I would see him next Friday at his house, and we would pick up where we had left off. He was mostly silent and looked to the ground, as the pangs of the fight, the worry of his clothes and his disregard for his mother perhaps consumed his thoughts. I pushed the grey button and notified the powers that were that we had finished. A guard came and took Justin away and clicking sounds signified the unlocking of the three doors through which I had previously entered. Reflecting on the visit, I did not have to use the panic button out of concern for safety, but if a button could have been pressed for fear of Justin's well-being, I would have used it.

Justin's attitude improved when I visited him in the detention center two weeks later, however. At his previous week's hearing, he spoke out against Lawon and Natasha and requested to be sent to his aunt's house where he thought life would be better. Natasha told the judge Justin was not ready to come home if he could not appreciate his home or his family, and the judge decided Justin needed three more weeks in the detention center to sort things out. Natasha spoke to me afterwards and said she did not want to keep her child in the detention center, but she could not spend all of her time monitoring Justin whose disdain for the home could result in another physical altercation. Because Justin was the strongest in his house and because he knew it, his will could not be impeded by Natasha and that caused her great concern.

Meanwhile, in spite of his adult situations, Justin discovered the world of Shel Silverstein in the detention center library. He read the book, *A Light in the Attic* and was searching for any of the author's other books to read.

Justin also was performing well in his detention center classroom, answering more questions than his other classmates. He made a friend from Danville, Illinois who was a fan of the rapper Lil' Wayne too. His friend resided in the cell across from Justin. These positives probably eased the burden of the detention center, but Justin could not wait to go home, even though it was not his aunt's house. He was woken up at 4 A.M. one morning when the guards performed a bunk search to discover any forbidden items Justin might have had in his possession. He had been rebuked for rapping when he was sitting alone in his cell one day. Singing was not allowed.

I asked Justin to consider what he wanted to do after he was released. During the third and final visit, Justin told me he wanted to try out for the high school football team. I promised we would continue to work on reading, but now we would use Shel Silverstein books.

It seemed as if a change was in the air when Justin was released two days before the Fourth of July. He was most excited about seeing the fireworks at Parkland Community College in Champaign. Initially, I was worried that Justin's time in the detention center would have embittered him, but it seemed to cause a change in him, perhaps acting like the gunpowder which causes fireworks to burst and reveal the impassioned colors within them. Who could have guessed that he loved Shel Silverstein books?

Natasha too was optimistic. A week after the holiday she said, "Justin is doing good now. I just told him that he is going to be the solid one and that surprises me because I was so frustrated with him a year ago. He would always talk back to me. He told me he did not want to try in school. He said he could do the work, but he did not want to try. But now he does not talk back as much. He listens to me. The time in the detention center was good for him. That's not true for all children, but I think he realized that he had no freedom if he continued the same way he was."

Unfortunately, Justin was now on probation, and his future mistakes could be magnified. If what he needed was a break from home life, perhaps the detention center was not ideal since it could only be delivered through delinquency.

As a mentor, the experience taught me that there was more to Justin than I had seen during our time together. I felt I had to make a greater effort to understand Justin's history, his family and his neighborhood if I really wanted to help him.

Chapter 5

Natasha

On a Friday in the middle of August I visited Justin's house. Natasha opened the door and said Justin was not at home. Seeing this as an opportunity, I told Natasha I was interested in writing a book about my experiences with Justin. Natasha was thrilled with the idea and smiled when I asked to interview her to get a better understanding of her life and Justin's. We stood outside in the summer sun for two hours on the small wooden platform at the top of the exterior steps. She explained her life's history from youth to adulthood. She was motivated to speak, saying, "I don't care who reads my story. Tell it all. Maybe people will understand what I have gone through."

"I didn't have a father when I grew up. My mother worked two jobs and there was a man who she was with. She gave him money, and he stole her money too. He was on drugs. I didn't understand why my mother would let him steal her money like that, but she told me I'd understand when I fell in love. But I didn't understand. I wouldn't have a man who would do that to me. It just didn't make sense, and I wanted to get away from that house anyway I could sometimes."

"I had Justin when I was fourteen. His father is six years older than me. His name is Jared. Jared couldn't read and still can't. He was behind in school, and probably had a learning disability like Justin, so he dropped out of school when he was young. His sister basically raised him. But he turned to the streets because they gave love where you did not have to be able to read - where people liked you for what you were."

"I liked Jared because I thought all the boys my age were childish. Jared had a car and a little money in his pocket. It seemed like a lot because I didn't have much. But he sold drugs and by the time I had Justin, he was in jail."

"I didn't want to have an abortion. I did not even know what one was. My mother talked to me about things like menstruation and sex, but she never talked to me about an abortion. I just do not understand it when you can have your baby adopted or even leave him at the supermarket and someone would take care of him. My grandma believed that aborting a baby will come back to haunt you on your death bed. You know, one night my friend was sleeping and ran out of the house screaming and crying. She'd had an abortion and had a vision of a bloody child running around the bedroom. I know too many mothers who would be good moms but can't have children, and other moms who aren't too good but have children they don't care about. Sometimes, it just doesn't seem right."

"Lawon's father is the same as Justin's. I had Lawon a year after Justin. Their father was back in jail when Lawon was born. He is in jail today and he asks me to write him letters about how his boys are doing. He is mad at himself because he has not been a better father and wants to help more when he gets out next year."

"My mother made me raise my children. She was not happy - me having them as young as I did - but she helped support me. I had to walk them to daycare on my own, and I still went to high school. I dropped out when I was seventeen because I wanted to take care of my children on my own, so I went and got a job. Now I know I should have finished my education back then because I could've gotten a better job now, but I thought I needed to take care of my children right at that moment. That is why I want my boys to graduate. Don't worry about the girls at this age I tell them. There are girls that are all hot right now, but you will be embarrassed to think that you liked them once you graduate. The girls that were quiet will turn out to be the pretty ones and the ones that you should like."

"I had Deron when I was eighteen and Randall when I was twenty-one. I lost all four of my boys after Mike, Deron and Randall's father, and I were fighting, and I stabbed him in his leg to defend myself. He walked home, and he left a blood trail behind. The cops followed it back to his house and made him tell them what happened. Mike knew he was wrong for what he did by fighting me and hitting me. He called me and told me about the police, and I knew that DCFS [Department of Children and Family Services] would come for me and that I might lose my children. I took my boys and went and stayed with my aunt and uncle - two very religious people who told me that I had to turn myself in because the sooner I gave up the kids, the sooner I would get them back. DCFS did end up taking the kids. They said I was not a fit mother because the knife I used could have accidentally hit one of the boys. I did not have any prior record, only a few reports of me and Mike arguing where the police had come. I was not charged with any crime, but I still had my children taken from me for two years. I lived in a bad neighborhood, I was poor and I was Black. Those were the three hits against me."

"Justin and Lawon stayed at my sister's house. Deron and Randall were put into the foster system. At the beginning, I was only able to see them for one hour every week, so I found out what I had to do to get my children back as fast as I could. My case worker was fresh out of college and that slowed things down. She said she had too many cases, but I was angry because I was only worried about my case. A non-profit organization and the domestic shelter I stayed at helped me out a lot. They told me what I needed to do when the college girl was not moving fast enough. I had to work as a cook, and sometimes I would bring the kids to work if I had enough time."

"I took anger management classes and parenting classes as part of my requirements for getting my kids back. I was in a general parenting class first, but I did not like it. They told us to do timeouts to discipline our children. That does not work with Black kids. My children did not even understand what a timeout was. I found out there was a parenting class specifically for Black parents so I signed up for that. They recommended taking things away from the children for punishment and talked a lot about physical discipline never being a good thing. They also taught us a little about African American history. I liked that. DCFS did not like Mike from the beginning, but he ended up taking the same parenting class as me so that he would be able to see the children. We are still married today, but we are applying for a divorce soon."

"I can understand why a lot of women lose their children in the system because it will break your spirit if you do not have a lot of support. Being in the court room where people talk over your head is hard. You don't understand what is going on, and it's scary because they basically have control over your life. I was lucky because the state gave me a private attorney who was very good. He told me that when I get my children back he wants to see me hold onto them. He did not like helping mothers get their children back and then seeing those same children in the system years later because the mother had lost them again."

"After about two years the judge said I could be a mom again. My case worker congratulated me on my hard work spent in getting my children back. But the head of DCFS told me how I had been a pleasant surprise and made him look like a fool by succeeding."

"DCFS expected me to fail. They didn't think I was going to follow the steps so they were not always pushing to help me out. I lost my children for two years. Justin fell behind in school while he lived at his aunt's house. He acted up in school and was always upset when I came to see him because every week I had to tell him that I could not take him home. One of my younger boys told me he was abused by one of the other children in the foster home. That made me so mad. I lost my kids for being a bad mother and they got put in a worse place."

"My friend just told me the other day that I was a good mother for all that I had done to get my children back. She doesn't need to say that because it is my responsibility. These are my kids, and losing them for two years made me appreciate them more. I did not like DCFS. I know I could have gotten my children back much sooner, and it really hurt my children in a lot of ways. But I know who God is. During that time I prayed, and I saw what he could do. When the lawyers and judge were talking, I felt hopeless because I did not know how I could have any say, but someone told me, 'Let God be your judge and do not worry about them.'"

"I have a boyfriend now, but I do not trust men to raise my children. I am used to doing it my own way. My friends say that is not a good thing and that a man should be allowed to act like a father. And they are probably right. But I just can't do it. I see them as my kids and anyone else is a stranger."

"I am working nights, and I get almost no child support. It is hard for me to know that I am not providing my boys the best stuff, but I am giving them a place to sleep, food and good hygiene. I do not like how children are cruel to each other about the clothes they wear. It is hard on the children but the parents too. I would like to give my children these things, but I can't pay for it. I know those things are not too important, so it's ok. I think my children know I care about them and they do respect me for what I do. That's what's important."

After we had finished the interview, Natasha asked if she could have a ride to the nearby gas station to buy a soda. We drove together, and by the looks of the patrons at the gas station, they seemed to think we were an odd pair – a young white male university student and an adult Black female community member. I questioned why such an occurrence was rare. The community and the university were physically close to each other. Perhaps this was an unfortunate reality of American society. No matter how much reform had been made, certain social constructs could never be fully undone.

The life story Natasha shared gave me a greater education than many university courses could provide. I found similarity between her and Justin's life because both were ready to escape their homes at the age of fourteen. I heard about the disappointment Justin possessed as a child when he could not go home with his mother, perhaps creating the belief that his mother did not care about him. I encountered a linkage between a father and son who struggled to read.

I also discovered the words of someone who was simply trying to be a better mother - not claiming to be the best or to have perfect children. And I thought it was a shame that other people did not have the opportunity to experience her story. I realized the university was a separate entity from the community, both socially and physically, and I found that mentoring helped me as much as it might help Natasha and her family because we exchanged our experiences that resulted from our differences. After that day, I believed that Natasha and I were friends as we worked towards the common goal of helping her children.

Closer then at that time with Justin's family, I gradually became more familiar with the Champaign North Side community.

Chapter 6

Changing Tires

As Justin began high school, social pressures became a bigger factor in his life. He was embarrassed to have the pair of beat up black Nike shoes that stood out for their age and not their style. He missed the opportunity to play on the high school football team since his physical examination was not received by the school before practices had begun. The promise of the summer seemed to die away, and the new school year brought the reminder that there were obstacles to overcome.

On Fridays I did not pick up Justin at his high school but met him at his house instead. When 4:00 rolled around I might not find Justin at all. Once, a green Chevy driven by one of Justin's upperclassmen friends dropped him off as I was about to leave. Silver rims were spinning and reflecting the sunlight out onto the street. Justin ran from the car smiling, embodying the enthusiasm of freshman year. Together we continued reading, and Justin read in entirety Shel Silverstein's *Where the Sidewalk Ends*. He found greater confidence in sounding out words. Still, there was much more work to be done, and while Justin sorted through the newness of high school, his neighborhood became more vivid to me.

The North Side of Champaign was a predominantly Black community. To reach Justin's house on the North Side, I would drive north on Fourth Street from my on-campus apartment. As I drove, I would pass the east-west running University Avenue. It was a road which marked the physical separation between the campus and community. The Beckmann Center was a major research center that bordered University Avenue, and community members remarked about the fact that doors only existed on the southern side of the building while a fence hid the northern side of the building. "It's like they don't want us to come in. The fence says we are not welcome."

Next on my drive, I saw two tennis shoes that were a version of St. Louis' Gateway Arch to the West for the North Side. They were tied together by their laces and draped over an electric line crossing Fourth Street. Further north, I often saw two Black men wearing bow ties talking with people from the neighborhood. I assumed they were recruiters from the Nation of Islam, a religious organization combining the theology of Islam with the liberation of Black Americans. At Fourth Street's intersection with Hill Street, I could look one block east and see an empty grass lot surrounded by a chain link fence. Seemingly ideal for pickup football games, the site was under a routine investigation by the local electric company to determine the spread of toxicity from a gas plant that had stood there 80 years prior.

Heading west on Bradley Avenue, I would cross a set of railroad tracks. Drivers would slow down to almost stopping on these tracks, as the bumps took a toll on the automobiles that frequented this street. The North Side was the older part of town, and it suffered from poor city planning. One could be delayed by the train for at least ten minutes, perhaps longer if the train stopped at that crossing. To avoid a train, the North Side had one underpass, while south of University Avenue there were multiple possibilities.

Some of the houses along Bradley Avenue were single story with run-down exteriors and unkempt lawns. Several residents would sit outside on their porches in the warm weather. A discount bakery shop was a central point where youth would walk for cheap sweets. A barber shop, hair salon, beauty supply and custom t-shirt store were the other businesses intermixed with the residences.

Having not grown up in that neighborhood, I struggled to look beyond its appearances. When I looked upon the people that I drove by, I viewed them through the same lens of poverty with which I viewed the neighborhood. Such a perspective was not useful because it was an obstacle to approaching someone on his or her level. In September I stopped by Justin's house and developed a more substantive understanding of his neighborhood.

Lawon, Natasha and her sister were standing outside when I drove up.

"What's up Dylan?" Lawon asked.

"What's up Lawon? Hi Natasha."

"Hey Dylan. Justin is not here. I don't know where he is at. He said that since he has a curfew [from being on probation] he does not like to come home right away after school. He broke his hand. Did you know that?"

"No. What happened?"

"He got in a fight. He was hitting some guy and then he was shoved and fell back and bent his hand too far back when he landed. He should be ok. We stopped the fight before anything really happened."

"Hey Dylan, do you have a four-way to change a tire?" Lawon asked out of the blue.

I did not know what a four-way was, but I gave Lawon my carjack and other tools. When I was pulling these things out of my trunk, I noticed that there were two white children in khaki pants and maroon shirts standing in the yard with their bicycles. They were talking with Justin's brother Randall.

Lawon placed the jack underneath the beat-up Oldsmobile that had not moved since I began mentoring Justin. I demonstrated how to use the jack after Lawon displayed some confusion about turning the rod without it colliding with the concrete driveway. I continued demonstrating until the jack had reached high enough to have lifted the right front tire off of the ground. Lawon did not exactly have the opportunity to learn through experience.

"Where have you been? You know Dylan gets here at 4:00," Natasha said.

I looked up and saw Justin standing with his arms crossed. A blue cast covered his right forearm. "I know. I had a detention."

No one showed any interest in his detention. Our focus was solely on the tire. A lock on the rim prevented us from removing it, and Natasha did not have a key. She took a crowbar that she had handy and created some separation between the lock and the tire by wedging the crowbar between the two. She could not push the crowbar deep enough to completely separate the lock though and stopped. Next, it was my turn to try, but I made minimal progress. Lawon's effort consisted of jumping and using the force of his body weight on the crowbar, but he did not improve on what Natasha or I had done. I warned him about shaking the car while it was on the jack, and he stopped.

Fittingly, the person with only one functional arm made the most progress. Justin found a hammer in a toolbox and hit the end of the wedged crowbar with it. Each hit created more separation between the lock and the tire. Natasha's sister cautioned Justin about hurting himself, but he ignored her. She commented on just how smart he was. I agreed and let the tradesman continue his work. I became an apprentice and held the crowbar while he struck it with repeated blows of the hammer. When Justin had finished, the lock was badly beaten but still connected.

Puzzled at the next step to take, Justin and I stood in the silence of the moment. Natasha asked Randall to ride his bicycle to the nearby Kentucky Fried Chicken and buy a couple of meals for us workers. A man drove by the house in a beat-up old car that had a fresh paint job and new rims. He yelled, "Hey," at Natasha, and she just laughed.

With reminiscence intonating her speech, Natasha said the man always drove nice cars, even when he was Justin's father's friend eleven years ago. Randall left on his bicycle to reach the Kentucky Fried Chicken. He would have to ride down the same Bradley Avenue that I drove on, eventually turning north onto Prospect Avenue. It was the main thoroughfare to reach stores like Wal-Mart, Meijer, Best Buy and Target. As a result, the traffic was heavy and Justin's house, which was close to these stores, could be glimpsed at by students like me who had to find a route from campus to those retail locations.

While watching Justin pick up the crowbar and renew his effort, I thought of Randall navigating through the heavy traffic to reach a place to buy dinner. I viewed the cars as intruders into his neighborhood, making his journey that much more difficult. I contrasted that with the vantage point of a driver who may not be familiar with the neighborhood and simply sees a youth riding his bicycle in an unsafe location. The child could have been perceived as ignorant and the parents as careless. It was a tension of perspectives as the driver might have seen a poor neighborhood, while the pedestrian saw an uninvited guest in their living space.

Justin wedged the crowbar in the rim again. Pulling as hard as he could, it seemed from the position of his body that he was sitting an invisible chair. A loud pop indicated the lock and the tire were no longer unified, and the lock fell to the ground. Natasha and her sister exclaimed at his feat. Mockingly, he asked me, "How long have you been out here?"

"Get over it," Natasha said, rebuking him for his pride.

I laughed at the exchange between the two, and my eyes were drawn to two teenage boys casually walking down the street. It conjured memories of my friends and me roaming the streets of my hometown during the warm weather months. I felt a connection. No longer did the neighborhood seem foreign. It was a place where children grew up and friends shouted each other's name. The neighborhood had its crime, its drug use, but it was something more.

That "something more" conjured the bitterness I had felt when people from cities would laugh at the rural town I had grown up in. In my life I had been asked by urbanites if I had taken "cow classes," and whether or not I "only ate corn." I was embittered by the ignorance because I defined my hometown through the people within it - the neighbors, the friends and even the known alcoholics who still lived with their mothers at age forty. I did not define it by the cornfields or the livestock within it like some from urban areas had done. The same was true for Justin's neighborhood. Amongst the environment of older houses, busy streets, and barber shops were his family's friends, their neighbors and even their known alcoholics. To define people based on the appearance of their neighborhood seemed a great mistake, especially when the people were marginalized because their neighborhood invoked the idea of poverty.

Justin looked at the wheel's four lug nuts that had rusted to a darkish orange color. Using a wrench, he made no progress towards removing any of the lug nuts, even though he tried with his full strength. I attempted as well, but it made no difference. As all were content to walk away from the failed removal, Justin tried again. Wearing a pair of sandals, he stomped down on the wrench with one foot. The sound of aged metal screeched into the air, and the wrench turned with a lug nut several inches. I used Justin's successful technique to remove the rest of the lug nuts since I was wearing tennis shoes and not his sandals, and we successfully removed the tire. Natasha then, after careful inspection, realized that every tire needed to be forced off in a similar manner. Unwilling to endure three more prolonged efforts with the other tires, Natasha said she would just have the car towed to an auto shop on Prospect Avenue. Justin and I left and continued our work with reading.

When Justin removed that tire, away from school, away from detentions and reading, I witnessed him excel in problem solving. Twice he succeeded in overcoming an obstacle when I could not, reminding me that even though he struggled at times in school, there were pieces of the world beyond school where he was more than capable. He dealt with heavy-hitting issues at a young age and walked around with his head up. I found solace in moments like these, especially when others questioned Justin as a person solely for his behavior and performance in school. While I understood the importance of education as a means of improving Justin's future, I also understood the standards that were placed on him were unfair. Much like his neighborhood, Justin had to be accepted for who he was in order to reach what he was capable of.

Chapter 7

Relationships

The month of November began with a few no's. Justin missed high school basketball tryouts because he attended Natasha's friend's funeral in Michigan. When he returned, Justin asked the coach if he could try out for the team in spite of his absence, but the coach was unwilling. Justin decided he would only focus on football and began weightlifting at his high school. A week later, the coach offered Justin the opportunity to try out for the team, but Justin declined, opting instead to disappoint the coach who had earlier disappointed him. I told Justin that he was only hurting himself and not the coach, but Justin seemed uninterested in playing basketball, so I considered the issue unimportant.

On the third Saturday in November I went to meet Justin at his aunt's house to help him with his geography homework. I knocked on the door and Justin's grandmother answered. She said Justin had not arrived yet, but he would arrive soon with Natasha. She invited me into the house where she lived with her daughter and moved to a blue sofa with short, cautious steps. When she sat down, she had perfect posture with a straight back and her hands rested upon her knees. She looked at her grandchildren, Deron, Randall and their cousin, with a wrinkled, stoic expression.

Justin's aunt entered into the living room and greeted me. We talked about Justin, and in asking about my plans for the future, I spoke of the possibility of becoming a lawyer. She dropped the pleasantries and instantly spoke her mind.

"You know we need good lawyers. I don't like police. They treat people differently. They won't arrest a woman because she has kids, but they will pull over a man for the stupidest reasons. They will pull over Black people for the stupidest reasons. You know I don't like people being treated differently. I believe we are all created by God, so why should we be treated differently? I raise my children to not be prejudice. I tell them to love everyone. You see. I let you into my house. I let you make yourself comfortable. I don't bother you. And I can tell that you don't treat people differently because you are here and because you are taking care of my nephew. But his brothers need help too. So does my son. You know anyone who can help my son?"

I told her about the Big Brother / Big Sister mentoring program with which I was not involved but beyond that had few answers for her. Her anger was reflective of the bitterness that was rampant in the impoverished Champaign Black community. Such bitterness probably stemmed from the disconnect between her experiences in Champaign, including encounters with police, that other community members were not as familiar with. I wondered if she had had just one friend from the largely white middle-class community, she might be less frustrated with the lack of connection to other parts of Champaign or the authorities within the city. Such a relationship could have been between two working parents who had more in common than they had in opposition.

Forgetting my idealism, I looked at Deron who hid his face behind a pillow. The phone rang causing his aunt to excuse herself and answer it. I watched the Nickelodeon television show with the others, at least until I heard the giggling of Deron who had escaped the watch of his grandmother and was standing behind my chair. Randall started to laugh, and his grandmother told him to be quiet.

Natasha came into the house alone. She had left Justin at her house and needed to borrow her sister's car to drive to work. She informed me that Justin was failing three classes. She also complained that he was sleeping over at his friends' houses on school nights without her permission.

"Probably trying to get in bed with some girl," his aunt said after hanging up the phone.

"Umm-hmm." Natasha replied. "I told them at the court hearing that he's doing fine, and he is. But he is starting to push it. This boy is getting on my nerves. He has to raise his grades or he'll be back in the detention center."

Randall asked if he could go with me to get ready for a basketball game as I left for Justin's house. Randall and I were driving north on Mattis Avenue, and I asked him about his youth basketball team. "I don't like the coach. His name's Randall too and he makes jokes and tries to be funny. I think I'm going to quit."

We turned east onto Bradley Avenue and passed by the Kraft Food Plant on our right. Looking at the neighborhood on our left, he said, "You know this place looks like San Andreas."

He was referring to a video game that was part of the Grand Theft Auto series.

"Why's that?" I asked.

"There's busses and cars and the houses. They look like them in the game. You get money for stealing the cars and for beating up people. You see that old woman right there?"

He was referring to a woman who was sitting on a bench in a winter coat. "You'd go up to her and mug her in the game. And you can get money. With that money you can buy stuff. You can get a big house."

"Who wants a big house if you gotta get it that way?" I asked him.

The game helped Randall to establish a link between crime and the appearance of a neighborhood. The Garden Hills neighborhood we passed was deemed the worst in Champaign by a local newspaper and feared by the

UPS drivers with whom I worked. Randall's observation made me wonder if we had been driving through a new, suburban neighborhood and he had seen a woman sitting on a bench, would the thought of crime even have even crossed his mind? The reality of one's neighborhood affecting the treatment he or she received appeared vivid even in Randall's eyes - as young he was.

We reached Justin's house. Justin, Lawon and Lawon's friend sat in the family room eating candy that they purchased from a gas station. Randall prognosticated scoring twenty points in his basketball game later that day. Lawon told me that he scored twenty points in one game for his eighth-grade basketball team. He was excited because he was asked to play on a traveling basketball team for the coming summer. He was regarded as one of the elite players in the area.

Randall won a free pizza coupon as a reading award at school and wanted to renew it, and since Justin had not eaten all day, the three of us drove to a pizza restaurant on the outskirts of Champaign. Randall was mostly quiet, being the youngest in the car, and Justin told me that school was not a problem like his mother had believed. He was failing his physical education course because he missed almost a week of school from a severe asthma attack he suffered and needed to have his absences excused by a doctor. In two other classes, he needed to hand-in his missing homework, and he would be fine.

At the restaurant, the waitress seated us in a red booth looking onto the restaurant's parking lot. Justin and Randall sat opposite me and each ordered an individual pizza. The two boys laughed at me for ordering a salad with my sandwich, thinking the meal would be too much for one person to eat. I countered that neither ate enough or as healthy as I. Like the light salad, the argument did not carry much weight.

Offhandedly, Randall asked, with a serious look on his face, "Do you hate reading sometimes?"

"Yeah. If it is something I do not like," I said.

"I hate it all the time," he muttered.

"You'd like it if you found something you like to read. You won an award for reading, didn't you?"

"Yeah, but I got third. I wanted to get first. But those two people read too fast."

"You can keep practicing. Just like your brother. He is finishing books on his own now."

"That's because you make me," Justin contributed apathetically.

A young girl, probably a year or two older than Randall, came into the restaurant with her family. Randall pointed her out to Justin and told Justin that she "is dirty."

Randall started to tell Justin what made her dirty, but Justin interrupted him.

"Be quiet. You're always talking about people. Stop doing that."

Looking at me, Justin said, "That's why I don't bring him anywhere. He's always doing that."

Randall handled the criticism well, eating and sitting quietly and perhaps thinking about what he had just been told. He finished his pizza, but Justin had saved half of his pizza for his younger brother Deron. We left the restaurant and dropped off Randall at his house. Departing, Justin told Randall, "Put Deron's pizza in the fridge. Don't eat it. Don't let Lawon eat it."

We went to my apartment to work on reading. We did so for twenty minutes and then drove Justin home. Along the way I thought about Justin's aunt suggesting that he was chasing after girls now. I asked Justin if he was dating anyone.

"No. I've been hanging out with a girl for awhile."

"But you guys aren't dating?"

"No. She wants to, but I think I just want to be friends for now."

He looked straight ahead and did not seem interested in talking about it further. I told him to be careful and reminded him that Natasha gave birth to him when she was his age. The possibility of Justin becoming a father at such a young age was one of my greatest fears. I knew ultimately that I had next to no control over such a thing though and hoped for the best.

Justin wanted to show me his bicycle in what appeared to be a bicycle graveyard – his backyard. Two bicycles were flipped upside down without tires. One was spray painted gold. Justin's bicycle was silver with a black seat. He had borrowed an air pump and a wrench before we left my apartment and tried first to inflate his tire by using the air pump. Justin discovered the tire had a leak after hearing the pump's air escape through a seemingly indiscernible hole in the tire's inner tube, and he used the wrench to remove the tire. He pulled out the tire's inner-tube, and, after actually finding the air leak, asked if we could leave to get a new inner-tube. When we returned I watched him replace the old inner-tube with the new one.

First, he proudly showed me the plastic, dice-shaped air plugs that he purchased using his own money. With the tire already off of the rim, he put the tube in the tire and then tried to fit the tire back onto the rim. He skillfully used a wrench to hold down one side of the tire while adjusting the other side to correctly place the tire. He tightened the bolts to reattach the wheel to the bicycle and set the chain back on track. He checked the brakes to ensure that they were not too close to the rim, but that they created enough friction with the rim when they were pressed. Next, he screwed two pegs onto his back tire and began to ride around the yard, circling around the driveway. Circling and circling.

I can only remember being tired after that day. I went home and wrote everything that had happened. Between the issues of school, girlfriends, the neighborhood and the anger in the community, what stood out was Justin saving half of his pizza for Deron, Justin telling his younger brother the proper way to behave and Justin fixing a bicycle with great skill. There were no awards, no report cards for these things though. Meanwhile, Lawon received opportunities for his basketball talents and rightfully so, but there was nothing comparable for something like Justin's mechanical ability. I did not know how he could be rewarded for such a thing. There may be only one no in November, but it seemed to be a recurring one.

This basic problem speaks to a need in this society. Social workers and volunteers, the "do-gooders," are perhaps the most willing to venture into poorer neighborhoods, but a multi-faceted approach is needed. Had a mechanic found Justin at this time and spent time with him, it would only have been to his advantage. He needed something he could take pride in, something where he would be rewarded for his abilities, and as a mentor, I should have done more to establish such a connection.

Beyond the problems of impoverished neighborhoods are hidden talents and abilities that have the potential for development. Not only should the "do-gooders" be working to fight the problems of poverty, but so should engineers, tradespeople, entrepreneurs and nurses work to establish relationships with youth to encourage their abilities. Somehow criminality and immorality dominates the perceptions of entire neighborhoods to the point that problems persist, and when the question of joblessness in poorer neighborhoods presents itself, academic performance and family negligence are cited as the source of the problem. Alternative points of emphasis are needed in schools though, and it could lie particularly within the business community to stress the importance of these programs for their needs of future employees. Record companies could be supporting music programs in the worst schools. Automotive companies could be supporting mechanics courses in the most maligned schools. Computer companies could be supporting information technology courses in the lowest-funded schools.

The underlying motivation is that people need relationships to encourage their abilities. The fewer relationships one has, the less likely it is that these abilities will be encouraged, especially if these relationships are with people of a similar background and perspective. What potentially hurt Justin, his brothers and his family was the disconnect between parts of Champaign's community that limited the types of relationships that were developed, especially considering that an internationally renowned university was less than five miles away.

Chapter 8

Mighty Deron

A week later, Deron, Justin and I were sitting at a fast-food restaurant, and Deron was showing me the inside of his lip. He was certain he cut it while eating his fries. I told him I could see nothing, but he repeatedly asked me to look. Justin laughed at his little brother, who had been quiet up until that point of our time together. The children's meal gave Deron a boring Trivial Pursuit card game in addition to the cut lip. All things considered, I did not think he was happy with his meal.

With Deron's lip still bothering him, we left the fast food restaurant and headed to his house. Justin sat in the passenger seat with headphones in both of his ears and started rapping along with his music. Deron sat in the back with his eyes focused on the nighttime outside. One boy was putting up a tough act, ready to storm out into the world. Another sat in the backseat, collected the information of his surroundings and stayed quiet. Deron just smiled when I asked him where his thoughts lay.

I dropped off Justin at the boys' house. He was attending a friend's party that night and since Natasha was at work, I decided to watch Deron until she returned home. Although it seemed another dreary winter evening, the frustrations of the effects of poverty were ably communicated to me by Deron that night. I understood then that poverty was not a choice but a lack of control over one's life. It was the mental toll taken by the constant reminder of one's perceived inadequacy.

Deron and I visited a bookstore and wandered the children's section. He was supposed to show me a book he liked to read, but instead he found his favorite movie, *High School Musical*, had a journal associated with the movie. He asked if we could purchase it, but I said no.

Disappointed, he wandered over to the train set hidden in the corner of the children's section. He pulled the metal trains around wooden tracks. I watched him as I sat on a chair designed for a toddler. Deron looked at me, perhaps embarrassed have such attention upon him. He soon became engulfed in the train set, and when another boy came to play with it as well, Deron was too wrapped up in his own world to pay the other boy any mind. Suddenly bored after ten minutes, he smiled and said, "You ready?"

We left the bookstore, and across the street, Deron saw the glow of a toy store. He walked in anticipation of all that could be found in such a place. He would not be disappointed when we arrived. First, he looked at bicycles and skateboards. He moved to the remote control cars next. It was a chore to get him to leave each section, but in seeing his discontent at being an indoor window-shopper, I wanted to buy him one toy to take home. I told him he could choose a little Hot Wheels car for 99 cents – probably the cheapest toy in the store. He chose a green car with shiny rims.

Meanwhile, many parents were shopping for their children on the Friday night. Few children were actually in the store, hinting that the purchases were for the upcoming Christmas holiday. One couple walked hand-in-hand into the bicycle section and stood next to Deron. They sized up a red bicycle not too different from the one that caught Deron's eye, and they smiled at Deron. He might have reminded them of their son or daughter.

I knew Deron wanted a bicycle, and my immediate reaction was to look to the ground and not at those smiling parents. Strangely, I was embarrassed that I could not provide Deron with the bicycle like those parents could. I understood then the battle that parents have to wage in raising children, dealing with the financial disparities between classes and having the need to develop one's own sense of security with what should be expected in raising a child. Still, no matter how secure one was in his or her own ways, certain experiences could always bring that sense of inadequacy to the forefront. The materialistic association of the holidays was perhaps the most opportune time for such an experience.

We walked to the check-out counter, but Deron ran to play a handheld game that was on display in the video games section. I stood in line with the tiny Hot Wheels car, and with the transaction transacted, was ready to leave the store as soon as possible. I nearly pushed Deron out the door as we headed to my car. I turned on the headlights, started the car and wondered whether Deron was oblivious to my confrontation with class. He was looking over his Hot Wheels car with his seat belt buckled when his usual compliance through quiet innocence gave way to an unusual effort at dissent. "Those people are taking all of our money. We buy things and give them money. They get the toys and a big house. But we need a big house too!"

Deron was a fighter. He deserved a big house as much as anyone, and even though he did not have one, he did not think those people who did were any better than him. To want a big house, was it materialistic? No. It was an effort to overcome a threshold that he did not set. Looking for fairness in the world, he quickly found that such an idea did not exist in terms of possessions. He wanted to alleviate the injustice but did not yet understand that it may not have been too great of an injustice. Rather, it could have been a blessing that provided him with a very mature perspective of diminished material expectations at the age of eight.

We next drove to a grocery store because Deron was hungry. He chose what seemed to be a better children's meal for him this time - a Lunchable. I paid for the second dinner, and Deron complained that he missed his mother and wanted to see her. I was too tired to resist and promised we would briefly.

The wooden interior of the restaurant where Natasha worked reflected the bright ceiling lights to mitigate the impact of the darkness looming outside. Patrons used the same wooden interior to echo their conversations across the crowded restaurant. Deron looked and listened to these things with wonderment in his eyes. Finally, he saw where his mother worked. Unlike any restaurant with which he was familiar, he glided over to the lobster tank to watch the strange ocean creatures move in the water despite having their claws banded together. Natasha appeared from the kitchen and asked Deron what he wanted. He pointed at the lobsters, wanting to know about them.

"Do people eat those?"

"Yeah. I don't like them, but I cook them," said Natasha.

After an extra minute of exchange between the two, Natasha said that she had to continue working but would be at home in an hour. We left the restaurant, yet Deron's excitement over seeing his mother, her place of work and what she did lasted throughout the entire car ride to his house. It was refreshing to see his strong love for his mother not grounded in what she could buy him but simply in the fact that she was his mother. He knew that she cared about him and anticipated her return home. Alternatively, such feelings made me question the disappointment Justin might have felt when he had lost Natasha for two years.

I had never seen Deron's house empty and dark. He turned on the hallway light to chase the darkness away. He was carrying his Lunchable in the plastic bag from the grocery store and wanted to eat in the family room. He turned on the room's overhead light. The light revealed the furniture of the room and the many roaches on the floor that began to scatter.

Deron lifted his voice to a mighty roar, "Get out of my house!" and he stomped at any invader in sight.

Whether the insects were scared of Deron or the light, I did not know, but at least five roaches did not make it out alive. Eventually all were gone, and while the roaches regrouped, Deron and I sat down on the couch as he began to eat his second dinner. The thought of eating, even sitting in the room made me queasy, but no other option was available.

We turned on the television, and Deron continued to eat. He was not embarrassed, perhaps because he knew of nothing else or because he had just accepted his house, imperfect as it may have been. Deron then decided he needed a fork and headed to the kitchen. He yelled a battle cry as he stood next to the trash can at the kitchen's entrance. Hurrying to see why he yelled, I saw Deron turn on the kitchen light, signaling the beginning of Round Two.

The roaches were not just on the floor. Some crawled on the gray countertops and others upon the whitish table. There were perhaps 50 in total. And stomp Deron did. Stomp. Stomp. "Get of my house!"

Stomp...Stomp....Stomp...

That night will always serve as my definition of poverty. While there were financial thresholds based on income, assets and debt, I concluded that poverty went beyond any monetary measurement. No matter how many roaches Deron stomped, they would always return. No matter how often Natasha complained to her landlord about the problem, nothing would be done. No matter how clean Natasha kept her house, there was always another level in that house that she had no control over.

Poverty is not some formula. Anyone can understand the mental aspect of it. I was reminded of the college Laundromat where I spent more money and time than I should have because the washing and drying machines would eat my quarters, fail to dry my clothes and stop working mid-cycle. There was no one to complain to, and every other week was a stress to return to the same place. Someday, I declared, I would have my own washer and dryer - just as Deron and Randall a week earlier had exclaimed that they wanted a big house too.

Poverty is ultimately common to us all - not exclusive to some. It might be found in the relationship where one controls another - such as a boss who exercises undue control over his or hers employee's lives or the romantic interest who influences one's thoughts and actions. It could even exist in wealth, when wealth demands the modification of one's behavior to consistently live up to a bar set too high.

Poverty takes a mental toll on those it affects. For the family, it was a constant stress that could act as a means to belittle their significance. But in Deron's excitement over seeing his mother, I knew that he loved her no matter the roaches or the lack of toys. The love was greater the environment, and to succeed as a family, typical standards had to be dropped as the family defined its own version of acceptability.

Chapter 9

Father

In the middle of December, Justin came to his house in a rush. He had just left a friend's house and running in the snow drenched his socks. He showed me a hole in the bottom of his shoe the size of the quarter. Sometimes I would take Justin to buy clothes that he needed. He might have a tear in his only pair of pants or lack clean socks. It was one way in which I took an active role in his life.

Another example was the time I brought up the subject of Justin's father. I suggested to Justin that we should visit him in prison, and unfortunately, Justin ended up being the most disappointed about the visit. I did not know what I hoped would come from the trip – only that it seemed an aspect of Justin's life that should not be hidden.

The day of the drenched socks, we bought Justin's shoes at an outlet store on the North Side. Justin pointed out one pair of brown boots, even though he was not interested in buying them.

"Do you know what rapper's shoes those are?" he asked.

"No."

"They're Birdman's," he said.

On the drive to his house, we continued the discussion of rappers. I asked him how many of his favorite rappers were in prison.

"Ja Rule went to jail because he had an Uzi, and they got him for having weed," he said.

"What is Ja Rule going to do with an Uzi?" I asked.

Justin laughed either because the answer was obvious or Ja Rule's actions ridiculous.

"Have you ever shot a gun?" I asked.

"Yeah. I've shot an assault rifle...A shotgun...A 9 [mm handgun]."

"How did you get access to those?"

"My dad used to have them. We shot them on the Fourth."

"The Fourth?"

"Yeah, the Fourth of July," he said.

The sounds of fireworks were similar enough to the sound of a gunshot to hide the use of the gun. "How did he have all of those?" I asked.

"He was in a gang before he went to jail. He was real high-up in one of them."

"What gangs are there in Champaign?"

"There's a lot. The Blackstones, the Vice Lords, the Gangster Disciples. The Goonies."

"What do the gangs in town do? Do they mostly sell drugs?"

"Yeah. One kid I know - he joined a gang, and a week later he had $1,000 and a gun. He got all of that for just sitting on a corner."

"High risk high reward I guess. Do you ever want to join a gang?"

"No way. I don't want to go to jail," he remarked quickly, as if the question was not a new one in his life.

"Have you ever seen any gang fights?"

"Yeah."

"What do you do? Walk away and act like you don't see anything?"

"No. I usually get in the middle and break it up."

"What?"

"They won't touch me because I have a reputation. People know my last name."

"It's pretty stupid to get in the middle of a fight that you have no business in."

"Champaign's not a killing town. People just get beat up. They might knock them out cold, but they won't kill them..."

"So do you like your father?"

"Yeah," he said without hesitation.

After a minute of silence, I asked, "Would you like to visit him with me?"

"Yeah."

Over the year and a half prior to that day, I avoided mentioning Justin's father simply because I did not know how to handle the difficult issue. But it seemed like a piece of his life, an aspect of his personhood which I was ignoring. I had to accept Justin for who he was, and to relate better, I tried to generalize his experience as one common to all sons or daughters. He was expected to follow in his father's footsteps by not graduating from high school, joining a gang and ending up in prison, and at that moment he was fighting against that supposed fate or destiny. It was that struggle of avoiding familial conformity, sordidly challenging that with which he was most experienced. It was a profound burden. And a child struggling to become his or her own person was, in terms of inspiration, no different for any youth regardless of perceived differences.

I spoke with Natasha about visiting Justin and Lawon's father Jared, and she was supportive. She smiled at the thought and said she wanted to come along - bringing Lawon as well. Recently, she said, Jared had written her a letter about his desire to be a better father when he got out jail within the next nine months.

We decided to visit the Hill Correctional Facility in Galesburg, Illinois on December 31st. I found directions on the internet. The trip there was estimated to last two hours. The Illinois Department of Corrections' website had a profile of every inmate, including the inmate's criminal history, physical characteristics and a photograph. I looked at these things briefly, and perhaps better prepared from the information, arrived at their house at 1:00 P.M on New Year's Eve.

Lawon was brushing his teeth in the bathroom when I entered the house. Justin was sleeping on his bed. Natasha stepped out of her bedroom and told me she would need a couple more minutes. "Oh. And Justin does not want to go."

I awoke Justin and told him that it would be a good idea if he went along. He listened but rolled over and fell back asleep. His attitude towards the planned visit had changed since we last talked.

I sat in the family room and watched Deron, Randall and a younger cousin wrestle each other. First Deron and Randall tackled one another. Next their cousin attacked Randall. Deron became Randall's ally and yelled at his cousin to get away from his brother. Randall told Deron that he did not need help and pushed Deron. Thus, the process would begin anew. It was the fight cycle.

Justin came out from his room and sat on the green chair to the left of the couch I was sitting on. He put his socks on his feet and said, "I don't want to see this gay dude."

No one was forcing him to go though. Lawon came into the family room. He stood over Justin and started swinging punches with the intent to miss by an inch or so. First left. Next right. Then...pop. Lawon landed an unintended, full-force right hook on Justin's mouth. "I'm sorry Justin," he said in a knee-jerk reaction.

Perhaps out of disbelief, Justin did not retaliate physically. He just checked his mouth with his right hand, eventually pulling the hand away to reveal blood from a cut on the inside of his mouth. His white teeth were now red. Justin told Natasha the instant she came into the room what had happened. Natasha directed him to the bathroom to clean up the blood. Looking at Lawon, she said, "You play too much. You gotta grow up."

And thus the fight cycle continued.

Natasha, Lawon and I walked towards the front door to check on Justin in the bathroom. He had a white rag tucked underneath his upper lip. Looking at the inside of his mouth, Natasha saw the cut was still bleeding and told him to come along with us, bringing the towel. She and Lawon walked out the door, and I waited for Justin, who walked slowly down the steps, resembling a beaten prisoner being led to execution.

The drive on Interstate 74 was long. Justin sat in the passenger seat of my 1996 black Honda Accord. Natasha sat behind me, and Lawon behind Justin. Lawon and Natasha spoke quietly in the backseat for ten minutes. Justin had little to say. He looked despondent - having a white towel in his mouth with red blood on it – and turned the radio to a rap station that seemingly cycled through the same ten songs every hour. A commercial played on the radio station for the Big Brother / Big Sister mentoring program. It told of the success story of one youth who was failing school until his Big Brother came into his life. The student turned his grades around and attended Illinois State University. Ending, it described the number of boys without fathers who needed male mentors. The commercial seemed to be talking over everyone in the car's head except for mine, as if I could be the salvation for a helpless situation. Embarrassed, I asked about everyone's New Year's Eve plans.

Justin's demeanor changed to excitement as he spoke of shoveling snow over the last two weeks to buy a ticket for a party at the skating rink that lasted from 7 PM to 7 AM. Natasha said, "I'm going to go to church. I'm getting to that age where I gotta start slowing down. Someone had their brains blown out two days ago at a bar over on Neil Street [in Champaign]. It's just too much. I know you'll be going out though. Campus was the place I used to go on New Year's Eve when I was younger. All the students are out. You know it's going to be a good time."

Outside of the car, the snow began as the sun started its downward course. The road gradually became hidden in the blanketed whiteness created by the winter snowflakes. We exited at a rest area and already the tires were losing tread. The rest area was atop a steep hill that required walking a set of stairs from the parking lot. In high heels, Natasha struggled to keep her balance. Lawon hooked her arm and helped her up the way. Justin and I were in front of them, trudging through the snow in the presence of the building storm.

Thirty minutes later we found the Hill Correctional Facility. We entered a small brick building that served as the gatehouse for the prison. Just as in the juvenile detention center, we needed the staff to unlock the entryway doors for us. A Black female guard sat behind the bulletproof window and asked how she could help us.

Natasha told her we were visiting an inmate and gave Justin's father's identification number. The guard made both Natasha and I fill out forms while Justin and Lawon sat on red-colored benches; as minors they had no paperwork to complete. Natasha and I finished our assignment, and the guard indicated that only three people could visit an inmate at one time. By default, I was the odd man out. The guard let the family through the doors. The boys looked scared of what was to come, as their eyes did not lose sight of the ground.

I could tell you many things about the small area I sat in for the next four hours. I came to know the life stories of several of the prison guards. The female security guard, the first we saw, was happy to have her family finally come together for an occasion that was not a funeral – a holiday reunion. A male guard was engaged to be married and had served in the military. He was happy to meet a woman who could hold a job, even though she could never remember to get her damn oil changed. One man mixed health and profanity in plain elegance. For example, did you know that, "85 f-ing percent of f-ing diseases are f-ing preventable?"

But I did not witness what went on in the visiting room. I pictured Natasha and Lawon, Justin and their father sitting together in the small room trying to reconnect as a family. Their holiday meal came from the $10 vending machine card that Natasha had purchased in the gatehouse. Natasha would later tell me that the boys' father indicated he was ready to change his life around. He recounted a recent experience when another inmate said to him, "Do you know who will be sitting in that empty chair next to you if you don't get yourself together? Your son."

He said he knew he needed to step up and be a better father. He was even talking of taking custody of one or both boys when he was to be released in late October if Natasha needed a change.

Coming back into the gatehouse at 7:30 PM, each of the three had a reaction that was his or her own. Natasha was happy with the visit but upset that I had not forced her to leave earlier. Lawon was quiet and collected. Justin was angry because he would be home too late to go to the party at the skating rink he worked hard to attend. "I would've made it if he wasn't in prison," he said, snidely referring to his father's situation.

Even though time seemed at a standstill during their visit, the snow continued throughout. I cleared the car windows with a brush and an ice scraper. Justin, Lawon and Natasha waited outside of the car in the nighttime temperatures that were probably below ten degrees; the doors were unlocked and the car was running.

"I don't want to come back here," Justin said. "Now I can't do what I want to do. I never get to do what I want to do."

"You don't understand it right now, but you made his day," Natasha said in an effort of reassurance.

"Why do I have to do something for him?" Justin asked.

Justin was quiet after that - at least for a good two hours into the drive. I just drove with both hands on the steering wheel, following the tire tracks of the long line of automobiles in front of us on the unplowed interstate road. Cars were abandoned in the median and on the side of the road. We passed semi trucks and snow plows and other slower moving cars. The radio station reacquainted me with the rap music I did not like. It spoke of the good life of parties and drinks and clubs - things that seemed disconnected from the reality of the moment. The damn Big Brother / Big Sister commercial played again, and I wondered how they would view my experience with Justin, who got punched in the face, missed his party and made a long, unwanted trip just from my bidding.

The rap music continued to play, and Justin and Lawon began to rap along. My opinion of the music changed when I heard it through the boys' voices. Neither was really trying to live the thug-life mentioned in the songs, but each was dreaming of a life that went beyond the drama that confronted them on that night. Natasha alone would sing along with the love songs - love being a concept which she might have lost faith in over time. She had just come from visiting her first love in prison, fifteen years and four children later.

In essence, I understood the rap music to be the blues music of the twenty-first century. It was medication in trying times. It might not solve their problems, but it helped them when times were difficult.

As the drive continued, I only aspired to get us home, and if I learned anything that night, it was about those blues because I found them in myself too. It was a night where I could not see to the next day, as if the night might never go away. I felt the responsibility of three people's lives possibly slipping out of my hands like the tires on the snow, but I resolved to tell their story that night. At times it was a story about the problems of incarceration, society, individuals, poverty and disappointment. Other times, it was a story of family, faith and courage. A father who had not always been present was contemplating a change. A woman with no reason to believe in him was the first to do so. A son was trying to avoid his father's path in life, but in doing so, might have actually been following his mistakes.

Chapter 10

Busted

On a Saturday night in the middle of January, I heard a knock at my apartment door. Looking through the peephole, I could see Justin with the hood of his black coat pulled over his head. Never before had he visited my apartment on his own.

"What are you doing here?" I asked since it was one of the coldest nights of the year, with a wind chill below zero.

A friend unseen through the peephole pulled a black ski mask off of his head. Another friend stood behind Justin rubbing his hands together.

Justin said, "We were just walking around."

"And you came here to get warm…"

"Yeah."

"Alright. Come in. What are your names?" I asked the two friends with whom I was unfamiliar.

"My name is Raca."

"I'm Percy."

"What have you guys been up to tonight?"

"Nothing. There's nothing to do," Justin bemoaned.

"What about going to a movie or heading to the skating rink?"

"Nah," said Raca. "Well. I wouldn't mind seeing that new Ice Cube movie."

"I'm really hungry," Justin said. "You eat yet?"

"Yeah," I said, "But we can go get something quick."

Walking to my car, I asked the two boys where they lived.

"We live in Urbana," said Raca, referring to Champaign's twin city.

"You guys have been walking far. I don't know what you were thinking."

The four of us were in the car driving to McDonald's when we reached the intersection of 5th street and University Avenue. Waiting to go straight at the red light, Justin asked, "Is that one Chinese place open?"

"I don't know. We can go look," I said.

I used my right turn signal and turned east onto University Avenue. About ten seconds later, flashing lights overwhelmed my rearview mirror. A cop car was following us. We made a right turn onto 6th street and pulled over to the side of the road and next to a gas station. The police lights continued flashing.

"Did you guys have your seatbelts on?" I asked the three teenagers.

"I did," said Raca.

Justin buckled his. "I think you might have gotten me a ticket Justin."

A Champaign police officer approached the car, and I rolled down my window. Another policeman walked around to the passenger side and shined a light into the car. The policeman outside of my window looked into the backseat with his flashlight.

"Do we have probable cause?" asked the police officer on the passenger side.

"Yep. They were shuffling around in the backseat when I was approaching," said the other.

Another police car and officer arrived and both boys in the backseat were told to step out of the car to be searched. The officer outside of my window asked me several questions.

"How do you know these boys?"

"I mentor this one," I said, pointing to Justin, "and the two in the backseat are his friends."

"Can I see your license and registration?"

"Yeah."

I pulled the registration slip out of the glove box. Another officer began to speak with Justin.

"Where are you guys coming from?" he asked after I handed him the documentation.

"My apartment."

"Where do you live?"

I told him my address.

"How long were these boys with you?"

"Not more than five minutes. They had just come over to my apartment.

"Does the boy you mentor usually visit you at your apartment?"

"No. I usually pick him up at his house."

"Where does he live?"

I told him Justin's address. Justin was outside of the car waiting to be searched by an officer.

"Well, I pulled you over because you did not turn on your signal 100 feet in advance of the intersection. Why did you fail to do so?"

I explained that we had planned on continuing north at the intersection but decided to turn after we had already stopped.

"Which organization do you mentor this boy through?"

"I do it on my own."

"How did you come to know the boy you mentor?"

"His former mentor graduated from the university and left for Washington D.C. I took over for her once she left."

"What do you do as a mentor? Do you just take them places?"

"Yeah."

"Are you a student here at the university?"

"Yes."

"What are you studying?"

"I'm majoring in computer science and minoring in African American studies."

"Is this mentoring that you do involved with your African American studies?"

"Yeah. I believe there is a real problem because there is no relationship between the North side of Champaign and the university, so I try to build relationships with the people in the community."

As pronounced as my reasoning seemed, I was not even sure what I was saying.

"Well Dylan. I am going to be honest with you. We found a small amount of marijuana in the backseat of the car. We believe one of the boys left it there. Did you know these boys had marijuana?"

"No," I said knowing that I was now as suspicious as the other boys.

"If you want to search me you can."

"Why don't we go ahead and do that."

I stepped out of the car. I could see that Justin and the other two boys were in handcuffs. The policeman asked me to place my keys on the top of my car, and he made me put my hands behind my back. He searched every one of my pockets and found a pencil stuck in the lining of my winter coat that took him approximately five minutes to remove. I stood directly across from Justin. We looked at each other briefly, but he turned his eyes to the ground as both of us continued to be searched. I looked to the ground as well. It did not add up that we were pulled over for failing to use a turn signal early enough. What was the real issue? Seeing the three Black teenagers in handcuffs made the answer obvious, and racial profiling moved from being a debate to a reality. Our treatment by the police was different on the basis of race. As far as I was concerned, Justin and I were both in the front seat and the drugs in the back seat. Why was one in handcuffs and the other not?

The police officer found nothing worthy of legal condemnation on me and asked if he and the other officers could search my car. I granted them permission and another officer escorted me to the backseat of a police car since it was cold outside. When I asked to stay outside, he insisted that I get in the car. Thus continued my preferential treatment – free then from handcuffs and the weather. I did not have the opportunity to speak with Justin. Our group was quickly divided by the police officers.

Eventually Raca was put in the backseat with me, as an officer in the front seat collected Raca's address and other information. Raca and I did not talk once their discussion ended. I was upset that he tried to leave marijuana in my backseat to save himself. He was probably upset that he and his friends were in handcuffs, but I was not.

Looking outside of the car window, I could see six police cars surrounded my car with their lights flashing. People drove past the scene looking at Justin, as he was the only boy still outside. Whether or not he was guilty, the suspicion from the police officers and spectators could not have made him feel good about himself.

Next a police officer opened my door and moved me to a different police car. The officers continued searching my car. They questioned me about my homemade MP3 player holder. They thought it was some type of drug contraband since it was shoddily made out of an old oatmeal box.

One police officer, having finished searching my car, approached the police car I sat in and said, "Here's the deal. We have had reports of three African American males walking around campus with a black bag and ski masks. We had a similar description for the burglaries that occurred on campus a week ago. We found ski masks on all three of the boys. We will be taking them to the police station. Do you know if the boys left a black bag at your apartment?"

"I do not remember them walking in with a black bag."

"Did they leave a black bag at your apartment?"

"I cannot say for sure, but I do not think so."

"Would we have permission to go to your apartment and look for the bag?"

"Yes. Did the boy I mentor have on a black ski mask?"

"No. He did not have a black ski mask. But he had a Zorro type mask on him."

"Are you taking him to the detention center?"

"We will to take him to the police station. If we cannot prove that he is involved with the burglaries he will be dropped off at his house - depending on his prior record."

The police officer asked me to drive directly to my apartment. He followed me during the two-block drive. To reach the parking lot behind my apartment building, I drove north past the front of the building to the rear. The officer almost knowingly stopped following me and parked in front. I met him in front of the building and let him into my apartment.

Making conversation instead of looking around the apartment for the bag, the police officer asked, "What are you studying?"

I gave him the same answer I gave the other officer.

"African American studies, huh? What is your opinion of what happened tonight?"

"What do you mean?"

"Well I mean the way things were handled."

"You found someone who had broken the law."

"But I am asking about the treatment."

"I do not understand sir."

"You mentor one of the boys, right? You are probably on the North Side a lot. I know we do not have a good reputation there. But we just try to stop them at a young age. If we can catch them when they are young, we believe it will stop them when they get older."

"That's not my fight. I cannot tell you how to go about your business. I try fixing the other problems. I focus on the social issues, so I cannot really say anything about what happened tonight."

"How have things been going with the mentoring? I mean besides tonight?"

"Things have been going well. His grades have improved, but there are a lot of problems that are weighing him down. He is dealing with a lot of issues. But I know he does not smoke marijuana or drink or any of that."

"What kind of issues? Issues at home"

"Personal issues. Teenage issues."

I tried to cover myself because I said too much. He was probing for something.

"Well we just try to stop them when they are young," he said.

Another officer knocked on the door and entered. "Is it alright if he looks around the apartment?"

"Go ahead."

The first officer and I continued our conversation while the other looked around. He did not open any drawers nor look too deep for the black bag. My laptop case caught his interest since it was black, but after opening it, he concluded it was of little interest. Another officer entered and made brief conversation with the first officer and myself. He asked me, "Do you always hang up your citations?"

He was referring to a jaywalking citation I framed and hung on my wall. Unfortunately, the humorous intent of the hanging did not exist anymore, and two of the officers left leaving the original officer standing in my apartment. "So you don't have any opinion on what happened tonight?" he asked again.

"No," I said.

I was frustrated to the point that I did not want to speak with the officer. A better mentor would have discussed and even debated the protocol of the night, but I wasted the opportunity to provide the officer with my perspective.

"Well good luck with the mentoring. It's tough, but I wish you the best."

Justin was found to be uninvolved with the burglaries and taken home later that night. I was recalcitrant for letting just anyone into my car. Still, in trying to give three young boys an hour of time for simple socializing, we were pulled over for a suspect reason.

Justin revealed the following week that the police had followed him and his friends during their walk from a basketball gym to my apartment that night. "We finished playing basketball, and the guys did not want to walk home, so I told them we could go to your place. We were seven blocks away at my old school. We got two blocks away. My friend said the cops were following us. There was a cop car going slow behind us on the street. So we cut across the parking lot to get to your apartment. We got to the street your apartment is on, and the cops were turning on the street too. Then you let us in."

The police most likely followed us from the moment we left my apartment. And it seemed that nothing could emerge from that night. A police officer could have chosen to be a voice of reason by suggesting that both Justin and I be taken to the police station or neither of us. I could have been more talkative with an officer who actually asked for my opinion instead of offering indifferent silence. Justin could have been more discretionary in choosing his friends and what he did with

his time.   But it seemed the stars of the night hid
contentedly behind the clouds.

Chapter 11

Last Chance

Within two weeks, Justin's innocence turned to guilt.

Justin entered the contact room at the juvenile detention center wearing a gray sweatshirt, blue pants and slippers. His eyes were narrowed as if he was defying the reality of his current situation. "What happened? Why are you in here?" I asked.

"My mom's friend was at the house, and she was yelling at me - getting in my face because I just got home. She was drunk. And I told her that is why I don't ever want to be at home. So she pushed me out the door. I didn't have a jacket. I walked over across the street because it was cold out. Then thirty minutes later, the police showed up with my mom. One cop took me and threw me against the wall, and I cussed at him. And he said, 'You trying to show off for your posse? You trying to be a tough guy?' And he started bending my hand backwards. I thought it was about to break. It hurt so bad but he kept bending it back. I told my mom to make him stop, but she didn't say anything. He took me to the cop car. His partner was sitting in the car, and I asked him to stop the guy who was bending my hand, but he just stayed quiet. So the guy bent it even more until I got in the car. I can't feel anything in it right now. I don't think it's broken, but I can't feel anything. We got to the police station, and I asked the officer why he didn't say anything, but he just stayed quiet. I asked for the guy's name but he wouldn't give it to me."

"So do you want to go back home after this?"
"No."
"Where do you want to go?"

"My auntie's house. I told my mom I don't care anymore if she says she's going to put me in here. I hate it at home. And she's the one who always get me put in here. The first time - we were arguing and I just left home. I had nowhere to go, so I went to my aunt's house. And I ended up staying there for two months. But then she came over, yelling at me for staying at my auntie's house and not with her. And she called the cops to bring me back home. When I fought with Lawon my aunt said that I hit her, but it was Lawon. Even he admits it. But they had the cops take me and not Lawon. And now my mom and her friend made me leave the house. They pushed me out the door and then called the cops. They brought me here."

In response I said, "I know you are in here for reasons you cannot always control. I understand that. I know you are not a criminal or that you want to hurt anybody in this world. I know you are a good person. That is why I am writing a book about you. So that people can see how you ended up in the detention center for circumstances you could not always control. But when I was writing the chapter about the night we got stopped by the cops, I realized that I had to blame myself for some of the problems. And Justin, you are not handling your things correctly either. You can control what you do with your free time. I understand that you are young and that you want to have a good time, but if you want to really leave the house, you have to improve yourself. You have to become a better reader. You have to take opportunities instead of walking away from them. In high school, you can be away from the house from 7:00 AM to 9:00 PM if you do enough activities."

He sat quietly, looking at the ground the whole time during my speech. Advice was ineffectual when it failed to deal with the heart of the matter. Five minutes must have passed. Then he said, "Mom, she just doesn't care. I don't even think she is my mom. I don't have a mom or a dad."

His voice broke as he said "dad." Tears started to roll down his cheeks. He did not look up. It was hard to hear what he said, but I told him that I loved him. "Your mom loves you too. It is just difficult to understand. It may not come across that way, but she is dealing with things that probably you and I don't even know about. So it is difficult for her. But she loves you too."

He remained quiet. An officer passed by the door and looked in at me. Tear drops saturated Justin's sweatshirt. The door buzzed and the guard who peeked into the window took Justin out of the visiting room. Justin did not say anything as the door shut, and the words hung in the air, unsettled like so many other things.

I was convinced that Justin needed to see what was in front of him. The people and opportunities in his life were substantial like his obstacles, and his struggle was one of accepting that which was given to him. Days when Justin's prospects seemed to dim challenged my desire of something greater for him, but the process was to be a slow one, and it might not even be successful. He was not a perfect child, Natasha not a perfect mother and I not a perfect mentor. But damn perfection. We were trying to make something positive happen.

I gave Justin's explanation to Natasha later that week. She tried to set the record straight. "He came home late on a school night. He was stumbling around the house and smelled like alcohol. My friend didn't want me to see him like that, so she stopped Justin and told him to go to bed. He said she wasn't his mom and ignored her. I came in and yelled at him for disrespecting my friend and being drunk. He left the house 'cause he said he didn't have to stay. He went back to a house a block away where he'd been staying some nights with some woman and his friends. She's almost thirty years-old, and she's dating one of Justin's high school buddies. She buys them alcohol and stuff like that. So I called the police and had them go to the house to get him out of there. Then they took him to the detention center. I just don't know what to do. I can't control him, so where else can he go?"

Where else could he go? On a Thursday morning in February, Natasha and I sat outside of Courtroom C in the Champaign County Courthouse. Justin's public defender told Natasha the judge would most likely allow Justin to come home after the hearing, but Natasha's input was the deciding factor. I asked Natasha what she planned to say when the judge asked for her opinion.

"Justin's still got an attitude," she said. "I called him at the detention center and he didn't even apologize. I don't think he's ready to come home. I bought his brothers all new clothes, and he was mad because I told him that I was not going to get him anything 'cause of the way he was acting. He thinks he should get things whether or not he does what I tell him to do. Well I'm sorry. I'm not going to do that. He's used to one of his friends who gets all types of new clothes from his parents. That's not the way I do it though. That boy's mother told me, 'you should be more affectionate with Justin.' How is she going to say that? Buying her son whatever he wants. How is that going to do anything? She probably hears Justin's version of the way he thinks he gets treated by me."

"But I just can't be spending all my time on Justin. I can't have him disrespecting me and making his brothers think it's OK to treat me like that. He has to follow the rules or else I am going to stop wasting my time. I love him, but I can't do much more. He needs to be taking his medication. When he is on that, he thinks things over before he does them. He is in control of himself. But his friends told him that they were 'retard' pills. So he hasn't been taking them for two months."

A doctor had recommended as early as elementary school that Justin should use medication for a behavioral disorder. Before Justin was in the seventh grade, Natasha refused it. After Justin used the pills for a week, she came to believe it helped him to make better decisions and encouraged him to take the pills ever since.

A uniformed police officer stepped out of a courtroom and announced Justin's last name and the time of his hearing. Natasha and I lined up in front of the officer and signed a sheet that asked us to give our names and relationship to the defendant. Three benches in the back of the courtroom were split down the middle for a walkway. Natasha sat in the front row behind Justin, who was listening somberly to his public defender. His lawyer was an attractive, five-foot woman with strawberry blonde hair, and she was wearing a pinstriped suit. The prosecuting attorney sat on the opposite side of the courtroom. He was a tall man with graying hair, typing away on his laptop before the proceeding began.

The judge at the bench commenced the fast food justice. First, the judge asked Justin a series of questions about Justin's determination to follow the law, attend school and adhere to his mother's rules. He answered the questions, giving the necessary information for the cashier to process the order. Next, the prosecutor and defender made statements concerning their respective positions, in effect preparing the meal in the back kitchen. The judge considered the facts and asked Natasha whether or not she felt Justin was ready to live at home. Natasha voiced that she wanted Justin to come home. The judge assembled the meal and presented it to Justin. He was to be on house arrest, only able to leave his house with his mother or myself. He was specifically told he could not enter the house where he and his friends had spent time with the older woman who provided them with alcohol. Also, he was still on probation, and in one month his behavior would be reevaluated. At that time he would either be on the path towards removing probation from his record or sent to a youth correctional facility. Instead of "Have a nice day," the judge gave the ultimatum, "This is your last chance."

I drove Justin and Natasha to their house after the court hearing. Justin was allowed to miss the school day in order to clear his mind, and I received a call from Justin later that night. He needed a ride to the juvenile detention center to pick up his shoes. Otherwise, he would not have any for school the next day. Rain poured for most of the afternoon and came down in sheets into night. The roads were covered with water, reaching as high as two feet in the flash flooding. Together Justin, Lawon and I rode through puddles which were really freshly formed lakes. While Lawon updated Justin on the new neighborhood gossip, the rain began to lighten. We arrived at the detention center and fifteen minutes later Justin emerged from the building carrying a black garbage bag full of clothes and a valentine he made during his detention. The valentine, he said, was for me. It was made on construction paper and had a cupid in the bottom right-hand corner. We returned to the house and the boys left the car. During the drive home I witnessed the falling rain impress upon the standing water, creating outward circular rings that grew until the initial force of the raindrop had subsided.

The fading rings reminded me that reading, for which I had pushed hard, had somehow become less important over time. The social issues that Justin faced occupied much of our time. He was unsettled, and I did not know how to encourage him to read when he was more worried about his living situation or his relationship with his mother. His "negative" actions stemmed from these things. And I believed they needed to be remedied foremost. Regardless, some notion of defeat still seemed real.

To help alleviate famine, one would first supply food and improve the ability of the famished person to grow his or her own food. To defeat poverty, one would provide money for the present and provide a person with a means of making money in the future. When Justin gave me the valentine it provided me with hope that he was able to trust people, able to believe that someone was concerned about him and acted in his best interest. I concluded the best I could do was to give him a positive, trusting relationship so that he could develop something similar with someone else in the future, perhaps in his pursuit of education, athletics or employment. On a night in March we had a battle where I tried to make this clear, even though the larger war already seemed lost.

Chapter 12

Dissonance

Randall knocked on my door on a Monday night in the beginning of March. He ran straight to the bathroom. He apologized for bothering me, but the Boys and Girls Club had closed for the night, and he was without a ride home. We grabbed a slice of pizza and went to the Champaign Public Library to read a book together. I drove him home and followed him up the familiar wooden steps to check on Justin's status. His court hearing was later that month.

Natasha was in her bedroom with Deron. When I entered, she spoke gravely with me. "Justin got suspended, and he got to fighting with some boy last Saturday. That boy hit him in the back of the head at the gas station down the block. My brother saw it and broke up the fight. That boy's mom came and yelled at Justin. She muffed him with her hand. He hit her back. Now, I don't want him hitting women, but he has to defend himself. I know that woman. She tells her boys to look for trouble and to get in fights. What is she doing putting her hand on my boy? She knows where I live. She could come talk to me. She could call the police. But she shouldn't be muffing him."

"Next week, Justin was sitting in class and that boy walked down the hallway. He said, 'F- you' to Justin, and Justin answered right back, 'F- you.'" The teacher told him to go to the dean's office. The dean was going to give him an in-school suspension, but Justin wouldn't tell him the name of the boy in the hallway. I don't know why he wouldn't just give the name. Sometimes he doesn't think. So the dean gave him an out-of-school suspension and brought him here. Justin just walked away from the dean and went to his room. There is nothing I hate more than a kid who doesn't treat people with respect. Justin made me look like a bad parent. I couldn't control him. He came out of his room and said the dean was treating him different at school. 'He's been out to get me ever since high school started.'"

"He thinks it's all the dean's fault. That school isn't perfect. The dean said they have kids walking around the hallways that don't even go to the school. They can't control it. How can they protect my son then? But he thinks everyone at that school's out to get him. I told him if that dean doesn't think you'll do good, why do you keep doing bad? You're just proving him right."

"He's over at a friend's house now. He's supposed to be back by 9:00. What time is it? 8:30? He probably won't even come home when he's supposed to. I don't want to send him to the detention center but I don't know what is better. I can't control him. My brother got put into the detention center when he was Justin's age, and he stayed in there until he was eighteen. He came out with a clean record while his friends all had felonies, and he was the only one who could get a job."

I told Natasha I did not know what to do either. I feared that Justin was too influenced by his friends and that he would continue to ignore her rules. I had to leave in May and wondered who he would answer to after I left. I could not believe that institutionalization seemed a viable alternative.

Natasha and I talked for the next thirty minutes, mostly about Justin's father. "He's supposed to get out in October," Natasha sighed in relief.

"He just sent me a letter asking about his sons. He wrote it on his own. He wants to help Justin most because he thinks Justin's a lot like him - no respect for authority. He says he'll handle Justin to help him get straight. All he wants to do is set things straight."

She looked at the time on a digital clock, and, seeing that Justin was five minutes late, said, "Yesterday I was yelling at him for the suspension and he started to tear up. You know, when you're a parent and you punish your child for the right reasons and you see them hurt, it still makes you feel bad. But I can't even tell if he's lying to me anymore. I don't even know if he's at his friend's house right now. I always try to meet him halfway, but now he's used to getting his way. He's more disrespectful than I ever was to my mom. I would never come into the house late on a school night. Never."

I decided to visit Justin's friend's house to see for myself if he was actually there. All of the lights were off at the one-story yellow house with a bass fish for a mailbox. Ringing the doorbell, Justin's friend answered the door with his father standing behind him. I asked if either had seen Justin. "Not tonight," the father said. "But we'll send him home right away if we see him."

I returned to Justin's house, and Natasha suggested I try the residence Justin was prohibited from visiting as part of the judge's order. She sent Randall along to help me find the house. Justin's brothers were always useful when I needed something in the neighborhood. Already at a young age they seemed to know where anyone I needed to find on the North Side lived.

We parked on the side of the road in front of a one-story white house. Shades were pulled over all of the windows, but light emanated from behind to provide silhouettes of the people inside. I knocked on the door with Randall by my side. A young girl with pigtails poked her head into the window like the doorman from *The Wizard of Oz* and asked what we wanted. "Nothing from you," said Randall.

Next, a woman opened the door. She was a white woman, probably in her thirties. I could see inside the house one teenage girl and two children sitting on a couch. "I am looking for Justin," I said.

"Who are you?"

"I am his mentor and this is his brother."

"One sec."

She shut the door. Randall and I heard people talking, and Randall tried to look through the now vacant window that the young doorperson had previously occupied. Next, a teenage girl opened the door.

"Who are you?"

"I am Justin's mentor and this is his brother."

She shut the door.

I might not have been the smartest man alive, but if Justin was not in that house, they had a strange way of acting about it. Eventually, I heard a woman's voice from inside. "I am not going to jail for you."

The door opened and Justin came out upset. "Did my mom tell you to come here?"

"No. I was waiting for you to come home. I went to your friend's house where you were supposed to be at, and you weren't there. So I asked your mother where you might be. You've got a lot of explaining to do."

The three of us left the car after the short drive to Justin's house. Justin did not want to go inside. "I'm not going in there. Look at Randall."

Randall was climbing the steps with a grin on face.

"He's smiling. He wants me to get in trouble. My mom's going to call the cops and put me in the detention center. You're just making things worse. I'm not going in there. I'm going to my auntie's house."

He started to walk away from the car and onto the street. I stood in front of him, and I put my hands against his chest and stopped him. I told him he was not leaving.

He said, "They all want me to go to prison. Randall. My mom. They want me out of the house. You look at me and you think my life is gravy. Well, it's not. No one knows what it's like to be me. You listen to my mom and think I'm a bad person. I'm not. You just don't know."

He tried to leave, but I stopped him again. "I know your life isn't easy. But you're acting stupid. No one wants you to go to prison. We want you to succeed. I wouldn't have been here every week for two years if I didn't believe in you. I know you can succeed."

He tried to leave for what was the third time. I stopped him again. Justin began to blame other people again. "My mom's the one who puts me in prison. I didn't do nothing but I got sent there. You don't know how bad it hurt to be there. It wasn't even my fault."

Few things in life are worth yelling about, and that was one of them.

"It's your fault! And until you realize that, things are not going to get better. What you did tonight was stupid. You told your mom you were going to your friend's house and you would be home by 9:00 P.M. You did not go to the house you were supposed to. That was stupid. You were thirty minutes late. That was stupid. You went to a house that you are not supposed to be at. You can get put into the detention center if they find you there, but you went there. That was stupid."

"You only listen to her side of the story. She lies to you and only tells you certain parts of the story."

"What about the time you said you got kicked out of the house, the night you got taken to the juvenile detention center. You didn't tell me that you were drunk though. Now, did you drink alcohol before or after that night?"

"I only had it that night."

"Did your friends pressure you into it?"

"No. My friends didn't do anything. I just did it to get back at my mom."

It was a bad reason. But it revealed how social stresses extended their reach to other aspects of life. Justin had ended that night in the detention center. It was a chain of events that most likely started with an argument with his mother.

I told Justin he would not have to go to the detention center and that Natasha would not call the police if he came inside the house. He conceded and together we walked the steps to the second story.

"The first thing that has to happen is for you to apologize to your mom."

"That's not fair. You didn't say I had to do it before."

We stood in silence for about five minutes, and he finally took ten steps and stood outside of Natasha's bedroom where she could not see him. I stood behind him.

"Let's go Justin."

But he just stood in silence again. Eventually, he made a movement, but instead of it being into his mother's room, he walked past the bedroom and into the family room. He sat on the couch and played with a flashlight he had in his pocket. I stayed in front of the bedroom, looking into the kitchen as water dripped from the kitchen faucet into a pan in the sink. Glancing over to my side, I saw on the hallway's railing a wooden plaque of the Ten Commandments.

"Do you know what the fifth commandment on this plaque is? 'Thou shalt honor thy mother and father?'"

"I don't have a father."

"You do have a father."

"He's never taken care of me. He's never been a father. He's never helped me."

"That doesn't mean he still can't help you."

"He'll never do anything for me."

"You don't know the future. You know my mom's father left her house when she was three years old and they did not speak much until she was fifty. Then she found out he had cancer and she took care of him."

"He's never going to do anything. I am never going to be like him."

"You were just telling me outside that no one understands you. He probably understands what you are going through better than anyone else. Do you think his life was gravy? He had a tough life. You know that. I do not think it is right that he has not been a good father. But you don't know what he has been through, and he might be there to help you someday."

He was quiet after I said this. In reality, no one probably understood him more than his father, and it may have been naïve to believe a change could occur between Justin and his father, but I had been able to become a part of Justin's life after almost two years. I did not know why his father could not do the same if he had the desire to do so.

It sounded as if Natasha was sleeping while we talked about Justin's father. I again told Justin he needed to apologize. "She is asleep," he said. "Go wake her up and I'll apologize."

"Who's the adult here?"

"You."

"Ok. Don't tell me what to do."

"You wanted me to apologize. I'll apologize. Just go wake her up."

"Justin. This is not my problem. This is yours. You messed up. You have to take care of it."

But he refused and sat there for another five minutes. Natasha then came out of her room and did not look at Justin as she walked to the bathroom. She returned from the bathroom and stopped in the hallway before heading back into her room. Justin looked straight ahead at the wall and spoke with a pillow over his mouth. "I'm sorry for going to over to that house and not coming home earlier."

He did not look at her and his words were not clear. Natasha, who had stopped to listen to the apology, grunted and went back into her bedroom. Justin would not sincerely apologize, so I conceded.

"Justin. Who bought you those shoes?"
"Me."
"Who bought you those pants?"
"Me."
"Who bought you that shirt?"
"Me."
"Who put a roof over your head?"
"Her."
"Who gives you electricity?"
"Her."
"Who gives you heat?"
"Her."
"Who gives you water?"
"Her."
"What do you give her?"
He was silent.
"What do you give her?"
"I don't know."

"There are only two things you have to give her - love and respect. When she tells you that you cannot leave the house, you have to respect that. When you say you are going to be home at 9:00, you better be home at 9:00. When you say you are going to a friend's house you better be at the house. And when she tells you to not go somewhere, you better not be there."

I left after that and drove home in silence. The prospect of Justin's father reestablishing himself in Justin's life provided optimism in light of the other aspects of the night that invoked pessimism. In existence, it seemed, was always some clash between hope and dismay.

Jazz musicians played notes that were rarely combined. They created uniqueness out of dissonance and showed that even in the clashing of sounds a new harmony could be discovered. The sounds may not have seemed musical. They might have been surprising. They might have been disturbing. Sooner or later though, the sounds became more substantive than any perfectly harmonic sound could. And those without expectations of how music was supposed to sound were able to embrace it.

I wanted Justin to understand that the right thing to do was not clean, pure and harmonic. It was littered with dirt and imperfections, and in life, one had to find the harmony in the disharmony. I wished that Justin could find something in his life, something positive which distanced the dissonance enough to make the music apparent. Was there such a thing? Could he find it?

Chapter 13

This Life Ain't Gravy

In March 2008 my car broke down and driving to Champaign to make Justin's court hearing proved impossible. Three days later, Natasha phoned to inform me that Justin had been sentenced to serve a year in an Illinois youth correctional facility not located in Champaign. He had been frequently tardy to school, received a negative report from the dean of his high school and had missed at least one appointment with his probation officer. The judge did not sentence him for being a bad child, but she said instead for his lack of respect for authority, as evidenced by his encounters with his mother, teachers and probation officer.

What was authority in Justin's eyes? In practice it seemed a contradiction. The people who were given power over his life did not deserve such power in his opinion. Justin told Natasha that he did not like his teachers, dismissive of one because he allegedly smoked marijuana. When Justin was put into handcuffs and I not during our traffic stop, he found another contradiction in the behavior of the police officers. Was it understandable for Justin to be disappointed with such contradictions? Yes. Was his method of lashing out against them proving effective? No. If Justin did not succeed in high school, he would always be subject to it. If Justin did not do what had to be done in the correctional facility and onwards, he would still be subject to the legal system in the future. The challenges he faced were like hurdles in the race of life.

Factually, Justin did not receive a sentence for thievery, drug pushing, violence or carrying a gun. The crimes which were usually attributed to dangerous youth were not relevant in this instance. He was a youth struggling with internal issues. He had his chances though.

And perhaps the seriousness of the situation could have a lasting impact on him. As Natasha told me over the phone, "In prison he's gonna realize that this life ain't gravy."

During the phone call on that Saturday, Natasha also broke the news that Justin would be leaving for the correctional facility on the following Monday. He was being held at the Champaign detention center for the time being. In order to see Justin one last time, I had to visit him on Easter Sunday. A time of resurrection felt like anything but.

Few snowflakes fell early in the morning on Sunday. Walking through the university campus, I glimpsed into the restaurants as families celebrated the holiday and the fact that most students were gone on Spring Break.

I drove to Justin's house at 3 P.M. Everyone was asleep except for Deron, who ran to wake up Natasha when he saw me. The *Transformers* movie was playing on one of the televisions in the house; it added to the semblance of emptiness since no one was watching it. Four of us left the house – Deron, Randall, Natasha and I.

A short woman greeted us at the entrance of the detention center. She took both Natasha's and my driver's licenses and said that we would be able to visit for as long as we desired since Justin was being sent away the next day. Natasha put her brown purse in a coin-operated locker, and I did the same with my car keys. The dull, cylinder block walls and gray metal doors which had such an impact on me during my first visit to the detention center now seemed insignificant. I had once felt sorry for any youth who spent time in such an environment. Such sympathy seemed frivolous now.

Instead of visiting Justin in a contact room, we had to follow the more secure method of communication over a phone as was customary in movie depictions of prison visitations. We pulled four chairs in front of the window, and Justin, wearing a blue jumpsuit, sat on the other side.

He pulled the receiver to his ear as Natasha sat closest to the phone and spoke first. Justin sat slumped in his chair with his eyes focused on the floor. Deron and Randall sat in the two chairs directly behind Natasha and me.

Natasha spoke for the next forty minutes and was there for her son when life was most difficult for him. She gave advice, reprimanded him for the way he behaved and told him she loved him. The details beyond that I cannot recall. Justin sat listening soberly. He was afraid of the life in the detention center which she discussed.

I tried to keep Deron and Randall silent. They discovered that they could see each other's reflections in the window that separated Justin and us. They made faces at each other for five minutes. They fought over some change in Randall's pockets. And when one boy was silent, the other would instigate him to fight. They managed to play in the bleakness of the juvenile detention center. It was no small feat.

At the end of the forty minutes, Natasha said in closing to Justin, "When you get out we will have a new house, you will be at a new school, and we will have a fresh start."

She gave me the phone to speak with Justin one last time. Deron grabbed it first and stuttered, "Good-buh."

He pulled the phone away from his head with a shy smile. Justin was looking at the ground as I began to say good-bye.

"How long have I known you?" I asked.

"Two years," he responded.

"I want you to look at me when I say this."

He looked up from the floor and straight into my eyes.

"I have known you for two years, and never once have I doubted your ability. You can accomplish whatever you want to do. You do not need me to succeed. I have taught you everything I know. And what you can accomplish is within you. Never forget that and take care of yourself."

He whispered goodbye and turned around to wait for the guard to take him away from the room. Natasha and the two boys were walking out, and right before I left, Justin turned around. I waved goodbye and headed out.

Justin would have a fresh start with his family, but it would be different for him and I by the time he left the correctional facility. I was to graduate that May and would leave Champaign. Regardless, we would try to maintain contact, and I walked out of the detention center that day with the belief that something good would come of our time together. Hopefully Justin would graduate from high school, find a job and live his life with some control of the world around him, and I hoped that I could do his story justice. Anything grander seemed inappropriate.

Initially, I undertook Justin's story as a means to document his life as a Black teenager in America, hoping that more people would reach out to what I felt was a disenfranchised group in American society. But I became a mentor first to help him personally, not some group as a whole. These two roles were competitive.

As I progressed in writing Justin's story, the problems of race and class which I thought would be highlighted became less important. It reflected a change in me, a maturation of sorts, as I realized that these controversial matters were secondary to the development of an individual. Individuals have to feel valued first and foremost. And race-based and class-based perspectives are ultimately about people seeking to find value in their own experiences, all the while reducing the value of others.

As a society, we should seek for value to be internalized within all of us. The effort starts from the moment a child is born and continues for the rest of life. Parents and mentors are important for this reason. So too is faith. And many of us are capable of providing a sense of worth for others that we are lucky to have received ourselves.

In closing, to know I became a part of Justin and his family's life means much to me. I have learned how to handle disappointment and find reward in it. I have learned that success, like many other things, is relative. And I have witnessed strength in a situation which is too often portrayed as helpless. This was something that Lisa, Justin's previous mentor, gave me the ability to experience. And I was excited when my friend Jason offered to mentor Deron and Randall while I prepared to leave Champaign.

Ultimately, I cannot know my importance for Justin and do not seek to overstate it. To judge by his biggest complaints, he thought of me as the guy who always made him walk when we went somewhere on campus, made him read every week and told him to not put syrup on everything.

I can speak to the fact that he helped me discover pieces of myself, however. While I was mentoring him, I also made comedy skits with my friends when I went home for my college breaks. I tried to learn piano and spent a great amount of time on computer science homework. But Justin helped me to see that I could represent something positive and worthwhile and even serve as a role model. And during our time together, I felt like I was doing something right for once. In effect, he made me feel valued.

Chapter 14

Final Word

I sent Justin a letter while he was serving time at a youth correctional facility. I asked him to write the last chapter of the book. He sent this letter to me in early May 2008.

Hey Dylan,

You would like me to witten something by me. Ok I have whit tough a lot since I was a lil boy I am try to be a man. I am get older am is year old I don't what to be in jill I has been in and out of jill for 5 year I can not do it no more. When I get out I am going to try to get me a job play football for my school and basketball and I get out July 2, 2008.

I love you Dylan and I want to thank you for everything you did for me and my mom and my borther and want you learing I hope we can see and talk still. Bye. PS if you can send me money place I am not eating a lot